God's Plan for CHURCH LEADERSHIP

by
Knofel Staton

 STANDARD PUBLISHING
Cincinnati, Ohio   39987

Unless otherwise noted, Scripture notations are from the *New American Standard Bible,* copyright 1960, 1962, 1963, 1968, 1971, 1972, 1973, 1975, 1977, by the Lockman Foundation, used by permission.

Quotations from the New International Version, copyright 1978 by the New York International Bible Society, are noted NIV and are used by permission.

Library of Congress Cataloging in Publication Data

Staton, Knofel

   God's Plan for Church Leadership.
   1. Christian leadership. I. Title.
BV652.1.S7   262'.1   82-3378
ISBN: 0-87239-566-9   AACR2

DEDICATION

To the greatest men I have ever known—the elders of churches where I have been a member.

IN APPRECIATION

To my wife, Julia, who continues to make sense out of my handwriting, and to Mrs. Linda Merold, who did the final typing.

PREFACE

One of the hottest questions being discussed today is, "What kind of leadership does God want for His church?" The answers being considered range all the way from the one-man-dictator style to the theory that the church should act as a democracy and make all decisions by a majority vote. Which, if either, is correct?

The Bible does not teach either extreme. Instead, the Bible models a balance. God does not invite persons to be the leaders of His church and then totally mistrust them with the decision-making process. It is far too easy for a church board to hire a leader-servant-preacher and then treat him as an ignorant hired hand who is totally mistrusted with even the smallest decisions. On the other hand, it is easy for a person to arrive on the scene of the church and totally mistrust the spiritual maturity of anyone else but himself. That leads to dictatorship, which is baptized in the theology of individualism. While neither extreme is Biblical, both extremes are practical and are used to a great extent today in the name of Biblical Christianity.

It is easy and somewhat natural to look at the environment in which we live and draw from that environment our models for leadership. We tend to look for the types of leadership that produce quick results. However, we must allow God to be both the Lord of our environment and the Lord of our time. His way, not ours, will change our environment and transform our emphasis.

This book enables us to understand *God's* way for leadership in the church by studying the *Biblical* teachings about leadership. The reading will be painful, for it will challenge tradition and will force us to look at ourselves and our churches to realize the need for change. This book does not elevate traditions (regardless of how long they have been around) to the status of the Scriptures. Scriptures must always be lord over traditions. Traditions must bow down to what God reveals to us in the Bible. We dare not twist God's Word to fit into the mold of our traditions.

The finest model of a leader is Jesus Christ. No one who has ever walked on planet Earth models leadership better than He. It is my prayer that this book will enable us to see that real and successful leadership must begin with Christ-likeness. If this book causes us to return to the Word and to readjust our attitudes and actions according to God's intentions for His church, my aim will have been accomplished.

TABLE OF CONTENTS

Introduction   From the Old to the New 9

Chapter   1   Who Is in Charge 15

Chapter   2   The Dimensions of the Church 31

Chapter   3   The Model for Leadership 43

Chapter   4   Leadership: Paul's Style 55

Chapter   5   Leadership: Barnabas' Style 63

Chapter   6   Gifted Leaders, Part 1 69

Chapter   7   Gifted Leaders, Part 2 79

Chapter   8   The Elders as Shepherds 89

Chapter   9   Specific Functions of the Elders 101

Chapter 10   Discipline in the Church 111

Chapter 11   Qualifications and Selection of the Elders ...115

Chapter 12   Other Gifted Servant-Leaders 129

Chapter 13   Structuring for Shepherding 139

FROM THE OLD TO THE NEW

I want to describe a group of people to you. As you read through the following list of characteristics, can you guess whom I am talking about?

1. They met at least once a week to hear the Word of God and to pray.

2. At least one person would read the Scripture and preach.

3. The people prayed regularly—even when not in the assembly meeting.

4. The members shared their income—at least ten percent of it.

5. The assembly did not permit women to teach men.

6. The members were willing to die for their faith—and many did.

7. The assembly had a plurality of elders and deacons.

8. The members sang hymns when they gathered together.

9. They were a covenant people—a community obedient to God's covenant.

10. They continually stressed the need for faith and repentance.

11. They believed in confessing their faith.

12. They immersed new converts.

13. They shared together in a special "supper" to remember their salvation. That meal included the cup and the loaf.

14. They believed they were God's people with God's Book who had received God's promises but looked forward to an eternal reward.

Whom am I describing? The church in the New Testament? No! I am describing Judaism in the first century.

The Jews met on the Sabbath to hear the Word of God and to

pray. One person in the assembly would read portions of the Scripture and give an exposition of it. The meeting was usually open for any male to speak if he wished. The members prayed three times a day even when they were not assembled. They gave more than a tenth of their income to God—actually an average of twenty-three percent per year. Women could not teach the men in the synagogue services.

Many Jews throughout history died for their faith. Every synagogue had elders and deacons.* The assembly included hymn singing—usually a psalm. The Jews were committed to God's covenant with a stress on faith and repentance. Confession in the Lordship of God was a part of every synagogue service. By Jesus' day, the Jews immersed every non-Jew who converted to Judaism. Once a year, they shared the Passover meal, which included the cup and loaf, to remember God's salvation of the Hebrew people from the slavery of Egypt. They believed they were God's people with God's promises, but they looked forward to an eternal reward.

This description of Judaism in the first century illustrates the point that leaders in the New Testament church must do more than coerce the church members to keep up all the external

---

*Although the deacon in the New Testament church cannot be traced to a synagogue official with certainty, several scholars believe that the attendant in the synagogue is a model for having deacons in the church. This connection was made rather early (Epiphanius. *Haereses*, 30, 11). The Greek word for that attendant and the Greek word for deacon have been used interchangeably in the Greek language. Moore discusses a synagogue attendant who is known as a minister (George Foot Moore, *Judaism*, Vol. 1, Page 289). This is the synagogue minister that is referred to in Luke 4:20. Although a different Greek word is used there than *diakonos*, the interchangeableness of the Greek word that is used in Luke 4:20 with *diakonos* in some other Greek literature causes some to feel that the synagogue servant or minister in Luke 4:20 is the root model for a church having a servant-minister-deacon.

practices, such as those listed here, or our churches will offer to the world nothing more than Judaism.

Christianity is radically different from Judaism. Christianity was so revolutionary that the Jews of Judaism killed Jesus and most of the apostles because of their Christian beliefs and practices. Jesus did not allow Jewish traditions to direct Him. He was criticized for the type of followers He was molding. The religious perfectionists asked, "Why do Your disciples not walk according to the traditions of the elders . . . ?" (Mark 7:5). Notice that the test of a person's position was whether or not he marched to the tune of the elders. That doesn't sound too bad, but notice Jesus' reply: "Rightly did Isaiah prophesy of you hypocrites, as it is written, 'This people honors Me with their lips, but their heart is far away from Me. But in vain do they worship Me, teaching as doctrines the precepts of men.' " He also said, "You nicely set aside the commandment of God in order to keep your tradition" (Mark 7:6-9).

What a stunning rebuke! That reply deserves closer examination. Jesus was pointing out an important truth about spiritual leadership. A spiritual leader's job is not only to get people to do the externals correctly, but also to enable them to have the right internals. "They honor me with their lips" refers to the externals, while "their heart is far away from me" refers to the internals. The result of external emphasis with no emphasis on the internals is vain worship: "In vain do they worship me."

The spiritual leader's job is not to baptize people into the ideology that says, "This is the way we have always done it." The leader must do much more than pass on traditions. Jesus said commandments were more important than traditions, and God was more important than the elders.

Does this mean, then, that we can do away with human leaders? Oh, no. The New Testament teaches us to "obey your leaders, and submit to them" (Hebrews 13:17). Jesus' reply does not give church members the excuse to become "lone-ranger" Christians who live independently with no submission. But Jesus' reply does spotlight the fact that church leaders must get their act together. No church leader has the right to teach "as doctrines the precepts of men" (Mark 7:7). No leader is correct when he sets up *human* rules that must be obeyed as if they were *God's* commands. The spiritual leaders of the church must lead in such a way that people do not confuse what they say with what God says. Further, whatever they say must square with what God says.

As we explore the meaning of this truth, we come to understand that church leaders must remain open to change and be willing to set aside their traditions and opinions for the truth. Leaders must evaluate their traditions *with* truth rather than elevate their traditions *into* truth. When we pass on traditions just because they are "ours," we are helping to continue that practice from generation to generation. It is far too common for people who grow up in the church to evaluate how everything is done by the way their leaders in their church did it rather than by what the Bible says. When this happens, we are restricting Christianity to our century instead of restoring the Christianity of the first century.

It becomes a vicious cycle. A person grows up in a congregation, seeing only the elders sit at the table to serve the Lord's Supper each Sunday, and thinks that only elders can sit in those chairs. This tradition, which receives no support from the Bible, is passed on from generation to generation and is elevated to truth. It then becomes easy to think that another congregation is in error when it may allow anyone—even teenagers—to sit in those chairs on Sunday during a worship service.

This same cycle becomes evident in many other areas: Who makes up the church board? What decisions should the church board make? How are elders and deacons to be selected? Do the elders have to approve the ministry and method of every member? What is the role of the preacher? The elders? The deacons? Do we have to have a mid-week service to be a New Testament church? What has to be the order of worship? Can the Lord's Supper come at the beginning, the middle, or the end of the worship service? Do we have to have Sunday School? Do we have to have a Sunday night service? It is easy to divide over these issues. But to do so is to divide over tradition rather than the truth.

If we merely pass on human tradition, as Judaism was so noted for doing, then it is difficult to talk with integrity about a *new* era, *new* covenant, *new* kingdom, *new* people, and *new* wine in *new* wineskins. The newness that Christ brings calls for newness in leadership.

How often do we study the Bible to find out how the leadership and the membership of a congregation are to be utilized? Have we investigated how the terms "elder" and "deacon" were used throughout the Bible to understand their roles? Have we taken seriously the Biblical description of the church as a family and a body and related the Biblical models of leadership to that? Or do we model our leadership after the leadership theories of the military, the government, or business and industry?

To be the kind of people and the kind of leaders that God intends, we must try to release ourselves from all other models except the Biblical ones. The church has always enjoyed a major thrust forward whenever she took the risk to study the Bible on issues she thought she already had down pat. And often she has found more secularism and human traditions in her "truth" and practices than what she had imagined.

We are living in a day when we must return to the Bible for a look at church leadership and structure, and we must be willing to align ourselves with God's intentions, regardless of the changes that may be needed. Unless we do, we can never move from the old to the new. Jesus had to tackle the same problem—of moving from the old to the new. The religious leaders of His day did not want to be freed of the old to find the happiness and freedom of the new. After all this time, Jesus deserves to be totally emancipated from the human tyranny that fetters the new.

In this book, we will study the Biblical principles and the corresponding practices that are essential if we are to witness the liberty for which Christ died and the life for which He arose. This will be both an exciting and enlightening study. At times, you will want to shout with joy because of the potential God has given to the ongoing Body of Christ. At other times, you may want to weep because of the gap that sometimes exists between what the church can be and what she is. But, most of all, you will want to study the Word of God with the openness to change both yourself and the structure of the church until we are all that God intended for us to be.

CHAPTER ONE

WHO IS IN CHARGE?

Who is in charge? That is a good question to ask, and it is an essential question to answer any time people are related together in any institution, business, government, school, industry, or church. No society of people can exist with peace and harmony without some form of government. Even the most primitive tribal societies understand this principle and set up their hierarchy accordingly.

In the military, it is easy to tell who is in charge. The sleeves or the collars of the uniforms bear the identifying symbols. One of the first things we learned in boot camp was the military chain-of-command, recognizing the commander-in-chief to be the President of the United States.

A recent convert who had spent some time in the military service commented to me that one of his frustrations about the church was that he could not tell where the center of power was. It seemed to him that in one congregation, the preacher was the one with power, but, in another, the board of elders seemed to be in control. In another congregation, it seemed to be one man who had no "official" status. In another, it seemed to be a group of women. And in still another church, there seemed to be no center of power at all. One can easily understand why he was confused.

Who is to have the authority in the church? And what is the source of that authority? Let us look to the Scriptures to discover the flow of authority that has existed from the beginning of creation and will exist till the second coming of Christ. We will look at the authority-base and at those who had delegated authority in both the Old Testament era and the New Testament era (in which we are now living).

THE OLD TESTAMENT AGE

God is the Final Authority. From the beginning of the Bible, we learn that God is in charge. No one created God; so no one can control Him. What He was He still is and shall always be. The summation of His status is focused on the sentence, "The Lord is our God, the Lord is one" (Deuteronomy 6:4). He is Lord, and He is God. When He speaks, nature responds with obedience. And after world history with all of its global competitors ends, the throne over all the universe will still be occupied by God—the ultimate and eternal power.

Step 1—As the final authority, God delegated authority to various human leaders in the Old Testament. Those human leaders were to represent God in what they said and did. God personally directed and inspired them. Their verbal word was to be heard as God's Word through them. That is why we read often the statement, "Then the Lord said to _____" (i.e., see Exodus 6:1, 10, 13, 28). In order to verify to others that these persons were genuine messengers from God, He gave them the ability to do signs and wonders: "that they may believe that the Lord . . . has appeared to you" (Exodus 4:5).

Step 2—God directed some of these inspired leaders to write down His communications to them:

> Then the Lord said to Moses, "Write this in a book as a memorial, and recite it to Joshua . . ." (Exodus 17:14).

> And Moses wrote down all the words of the Lord . . . (24:4).

> Then the Lord said to Moses, "Write down these words . . ." (34:27).

> So Moses wrote this law and gave it to the priests . . . (Deut. 31:9).

> And it came about, when Moses finished writing the words of this law in a book until they were complete, that Moses commanded the Levites, . . . "Take this book of the law and place it beside the ark of the covenant . . ." (Deut. 31:24-26).

> And Joshua wrote these words in the book of the law of God (Joshua 24:26).

Then Samuel . . . wrote them in the book . . . (1 Samuel 10:25).

Thus says the Lord, the God of Israel, "Write all the words which I have spoken to you in a book" (Jeremiah 30:2).

Take a scroll and write on it all the words which I have spoken to you concerning Israel, and concerning Judah, and concerning all the nations, from the day I first spoke to you, from the days of Josiah, even to this day. . . . Then Jeremiah called Baruch . . . , and Baruch wrote at the dictation of Jeremiah all the words of the Lord, which He had spoken to him, on a scroll (Jeremiah 36:2-4).

Step 3—After the death of these inspired leaders, this written Word of God became the authority for God's people. Those leaders who were not personally directed and inspired by God (such as the priests, scribes, rulers, and elders) were to put themselves under the guidance of the written Word. That written Word was to be their source of direction and inspiration from God. These non-inspired leaders did not receive from God the ability to do signs and wonders.

We can understand how the Jewish people regarded the Word of God to be the authority when we read the following verses (among others): "What was spoken by the Lord through the prophet . . ." (Matthew 1:22); "That which was spoken through Jeremiah . . ." (Matthew 2:17); "What was spoken of through the prophet Joel" (Acts 2:16). Notice the use of the word "through" *(dia)* in each of the verses. The Word was spoken *through* the human leader, not *by* him *(upo)*. Because each man spoke and wrote as he was moved by the Spirit of God, we read:

All Scripture is inspired by God and profitable for teaching, for reproof, for correction, for training in righteousness; that the man of God may be adequate, equipped for every good work (2 Timothy 3:16, 17).

In fact, the written Word of God was seen as having so much the authority of God that sometimes the Jews interchanged the words "God" and "Scripture." When the Scriptures spoke, they understood that God was speaking:

> For the Scripture says to Pharaoh, "For this very purpose I raised you up, to demonstrate My power in you, and that My name might be proclaimed throughout the whole earth" (Romans 9:17).

When this statement was made to Pharaoh, the Scripture had not yet been written; but for the Jews, what God said was Scripture.

> And the Scripture, foreseeing that God would justify the Gentiles by faith, preached the gospel beforehand to Abraham, saying, 'All the nations shall be blessed in you' (Galatians 3:8).

In the time of Abraham, however, there was no written Scripture. Genesis clarifies what is meant by saying, "Now the Lord said to Abram . . ." (Genesis 12:1).

It is clear that the Scripture was seen to be the very Word of God, even though spoken and written through men. After God's directly inspired leaders died, God's subsequent leaders saw that God's on-going authority was communicated through the written Word.

Although some of God's leaders who were under the Old Covenant added oral tradition to what was written, and elevated their oral law to the same status as God's written Word, they were wrong in doing so. Jesus criticized some leaders in His day for grabbing for authority by making their words as binding as God's written Word (Mark 7:1-7). No uninspired human being has a right to demand obedience to his words in the equal degree as obedience to God's written Word.

In summary, the flow of authority in the Old Testament could be charted like the chart on page 19.

THE NEW TESTAMENT AGE

God still remained as the final authority in the time of the New Testament. Jesus was equal with God, having participated in the creation (John 1:2, 3).

Step 1—Even though Jesus was in the form of God (Philippians 2:6; John 1:1), He emptied Himself and was born in the

GOD
Supreme Authority

INSPIRED PROPHETS

INSPIRED WRITINGS
Scripture of the O.T.

GOD'S PEOPLE
under authority of all the above

likeness of men (Philippians 2:7). Being God in flesh, He did not come to destroy the Old Testament writings (Scripture), but to fulfill them (Matthew 5:17: Galatians 3:24-26). While walking around in human flesh, Jesus did not by-pass the written Word of God. He declared, "It is written," and made God's Word the authoritative direction for His life (Matthew 4:4). He even declared that Scripture could not be broken (John 10:35).

Although He never disobeyed the Old Testament writings, He did go beyond them by ushering in God's New Covenant. Consequently, what He did and what He said not only fulfilled the Old, but introduced the New. The introduction of the New was done in complete accordance with God's authority and direction; thus, the New Testament is God's new agreement with His people.

The following verses show clearly that Jesus acted and spoke under the authority of His Father:

> I can do nothing on My own initiative (John 5:30).

> For I have come down from heaven, not to do My own will, but the will of Him who sent Me (John 6:38).

My teaching is not Mine, but His who sent Me (John 7:16).

The things which I heard from Him, these I speak to the world (John 8:26).

When you lift up the Son of Man, then you will know that I am He, and I do nothing on My own initiative, but I speak these things as the Father taught Me (John 8:28).

For I did not speak on My own initiative, but the Father Himself who sent Me has given Me commandment, what to say, and what to speak (John 12:49).

The word which you hear is not Mine, but the Father's who sent Me (John 14:24).

God also verified that Jesus acted under His authority by giving Him power to work signs and wonders. John wrote his Gospel to demonstrate that (John wrote his Gospel to demonstrate that (John 20:30, 31), Peter spoke of that fact on the day of Pentecost:

Men of Israel, listen to these words: Jesus the Nazarene, a man attested to you by God with miracles and wonders and signs which God performed through Him in your midst, just as you yourselves know (Acts 2:22).

This verification was important for the people's awareness because God never gave anyone signs and wonders whom He had not also inspired to speak His Words—Words that became Scripture—and certainly Jesus' Words were to become Scripture.

Step 2—Because of Jesus' complete submission to the authority of God—submission which took Jesus to the cross (Philippians 2:6-8)—God gave to Jesus

the name which is above every name, that at the name of Jesus every knee should bow, of those who are in heaven, and on earth, and under the earth, and that every tongue should confess that Jesus Christ is Lord, to the glory of God the Father (Philippians 2:9-11).

Along with a name of power and authority and exaltation, He also gave Jesus the headship of the church (Ephesians 1:22). The church is not a freak. It is neither headless nor multi-headed. Jesus is the head of the church; any human leader who tries to be the head of the church as a whole or of any local congregation has set himself up as a competitor to Christ.

Step 3—With this delegated authority from God, Jesus commissioned apostles, promising that these men would be inspired by God:

> But when He, the Spirit of truth, comes, He will guide you into *all* the truth; for He will not speak on His own initiative, but what ever He hears, He will speak; and He will disclose to you what is to come (John 16:13).

An apostle is someone sent out on a mission by a higher authority. While on that mission, he is to do the bidding of his higher authority, and he is to speak the message of that authority. There could have been no such thing as a true apostle who was independent and autonomous.

When the Spirit of God came upon the apostles on the day of Pentecost, they began to speak inspired words from God. To verify that they were speaking God's words, God gave them the ability to do signs and wonders. Early Christians understood this fact clearly. In the earliest days of the church, we read that the people "were continually devoting themselves to the apostles' teaching and to fellowship, to the breaking of the bread and to prayer" (Acts 2:42). The apostles also understood that their preaching was the Word of God and admitted it: "It is not desirable for us to neglect the word of God . . ."(Acts 6:2).

Later, Jesus selected another apostle named Saul/Paul, taught him inspired words, and gave him the ability to do signs and wonders:

> But the Lord said to him, 'Go, for he is a chosen instrument of Mine, to bear My name before the Gentiles and kings and the sons of Israel; for I will show him how much he must suffer for My name's sake (Acts 9:15, 16).

For I neither received it from man, nor was I taught it, but I received it through a revelation of Jesus Christ (Galatians 1:12).

Boasting is necessary, though it is not profitable; but I will go on to visions and revelations of the Lord (2 Corinthians 12:1).

Therefore they spent a long time there speaking boldly with reliance upon the Lord, who was bearing witness to the word of His grace, granting that signs and wonders be done by their hands (Acts 14:3).

When Paul spoke and wrote as an apostle, he spoke and wrote the inspired Word of God:

And for this reason we also constantly thank God that when you received from us the word of God's message, you accepted it not as the word of men, but for what it really is, the word of God, which also performs its work in you who believed (1 Thessalonians 2:13).

Step 4—As Christianity spread, God commissioned some others to be His inspired spokesmen. They were not apostles, but prophets.

Now we have received, not the spirit of the world, but the Spirit who is from God, that we might know the things freely given to us by God, which things we also speak, not in words taught by human wisdom, but in those taught by the Spirit, combining spiritual thoughts with spiritual words (1 Corinthians 2:12, 13).

But one who prophesies speaks to men for edification and exhortation and consolation. One who speaks in a tongue edifies himself; but one who prophesies edifies the church (1 Corinthians 14:3, 4).

And let two or three prophets speak, and let the others pass judgment. But if a revelation is made to another who is seated, let the first keep silent. For you can all prophesy one by one, so that all may learn and all may be exhorted; and the spirits of prophets are subject to prophets; for God is not a God of confusion but of peace, as in all the churches of the saints (1 Corinthians 14:29-33).

God gave these prophets the ability to do signs and wonders to verify that they were speaking His message:

> . . . After it was at the first spoken through the Lord, it was confirmed to us by *those who heard,* God also bearing witness with them, both by signs and wonders and by various miracles and by gifts of the Holy Spirit according to His own will (Hebrews 2:3, 4).

Thus Mark, Luke, James, and Jude wrote inspired words as well as some of the apostles.

Step 5—God's inspired words through the apostles and prophets were written down and became the New Testament. Every leader who lives after the days of the New Testament apostles and prophets are to put themselves directly underneath the authority of these writings (Scripture).

No human has the right to add or subtract from these writings, and no person has a right to claim to be a modern-day apostle or prophet. To prevent such claims, God inspired Paul to describe the church as God's household "having been built upon the foundation of the apostles and prophets, Christ Jesus Himself being the corner stone" (Ephesians 2:19, 20). Notice that the foundation for the church was already in place by the time Paul wrote the Ephesian letter. There were to be no more inspired apostles and prophets. Others who claimed such positions would be false apostles and prophets. The true apostles and prophets had much to say about the false claims:

> For such men are false apostles, deceitful workers, disguising themselves as apostles of Christ. And no wonder, for even Satan disguises himself as an angel of light. Therefore it is not surprising if his servants also disguise themselves as servants of righteousness; whose end shall be according to their deeds (2 Corinthians 11:13-15).

> But false prophets also arose among the people, just as there will also be false teachers among you, who will secretly introduce destructive heresies, even denying the Master who bought them, bringing swift destruction upon themselves. And many will follow their sensuality, and because of them the way of the truth will be maligned; and in their greed they will exploit you

24

with false words; their judgment from long ago is not idle, and their destruction is not asleep (2 Peter 2:1-3).

The faith has already been "once for all delivered to the saints" (Jude 3). There are no new revelations today.

The flow of authority for the New Testament church today would be charted as follows:

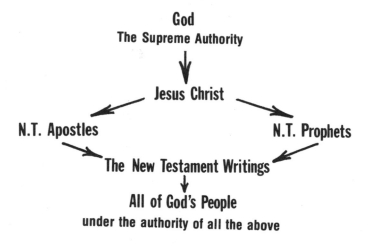

God
The Supreme Authority

Jesus Christ

N.T. Apostles

N.T. Prophets

The New Testament Writings

All of God's People
under the authority of all the above

Every Christian, whether he is in a leadership position in the church or not, must align himself under the Word of God. To do that is to remain connected to our Head, Jesus Christ—who is connected to our final authority, God—and is to stand firm upon the foundation of the New Testament apostles and prophets.

AUTHORITY OR AUTHORITARIANISM

Before we discuss in detail the leaders who are in the church today, we must arrive at some understanding of what type of authority has been delegated to us by God and Jesus under the guidance of the Scripture.

There is a vast difference between having some authority and expressing authoritarianism in the church. To have authority is to have influence, but to be an authoritarian is to demand blind submssion. Having authority in the church does not necessarily mean a person or group has all the power. In fact, in the church, those who have authority are equal to the members, not superior. But when authoritarianism reigns, power is concentrated in one leader, such as a ruling elder or preacher, or in a group of leaders, such as the official board. While a person with authority is responsible to the people, an authoritarian feels he is not responsible to the congregation. While a person with legitimate authority is a vessel through whom the influence of the Head, Jesus, flows, the authoritarian is the total influence and power. He is not just a container; he is also the content.

This difference was beautifully illustrated when Don Earl Boatman, who had been President of Ozark Bible College for twenty-five years, was asked how he handled the lines of authority between himself and Seth Wilson, who had been Academic Dean for thirty-five years. Mr. Boatman replied, "We do not function in the realm of authority, but of responsibilities."

That answer may sound like a cop-out at first, for surely someone has to make final decisions. And, of course, someone does. But there is a vast difference between making final decisions in the fellowship of a community and making all the decisions in the form of commands. There is a vast difference between giving someone responsibility with the authority to carry it out and giving responsibility while retaining authority in one man or a board. There is a vast difference between being a catalyst and being a commander.

The Apostles and Authority. It is interesting to note that the Greek word for authority is never used in the New Testament for anyone *in the church* except the apostles. But it is even more interesting to note how the apostles handled their authority.

There are two ways to handle authority—with humility or with arrogance. Humility will utilize *agape* love, but arrogance will utilize authoritarianism. The apostles had authority, but they never claimed to be the bosses over subordinates. They handled their authority with humility. As an apostle, Paul could have ordered Barnabas not to take John Mark with him, but he didn't. He allowed Barnabas the freedom to live out his ideas (Acts 15:36-41). As apostles, Paul and Peter could have squelched any discussion about whether or not circumcision was essential to salvation, but they did not. Instead of forming their own apostolic council to dictate conclusions, they agreed to have a conference with the church (Acts 15). As an apostle, Paul could have demanded many rights, but he refused to do so (1 Corinthians 9). He could have ordered Philemon to take back Onesimus, but he did not (Philemon 8-20). As an apostle, Peter could have declared that he was free from the need of correction, but he took correction well (Galatians 2:11-21). As an apostle, Peter could have become unglued when Christians took issue with him, but he did not (Acts 11:2).

The apostles took the people in the congregations seriously and acted with the knowledge and consent of the congregations in matters in which there was not a clear command from the Lord (Acts 1:15; 4:23; 6:3; 14:27; 15; 21:17-26). Why didn't these men act like authoritarians? Because they knew that Jesus was the holder of all authority (Colossians 2:10), and they were seeking to be vessels of Jesus' love.

Leadership with Equality. Because of the world within which we live, the issue of authority in the church is a hard concept to understand from God's point of view. To God, authority has *nothing* to do with superiority. The members of the church at Corinth had a tough time understanding that, and so do we. Paul emphasized *equality with differences* when he wrote:

> Now there are *varieties* of gifts, but the *same* Spirit. And there are *varieties* of ministries, and the *same* Lord. And there are *varieties* of effects, but the *same* God who works all things in all persons (1 Corinthians 12:4-6).

Notice the repetition of the words *varieties* and *same*. The varieties of human abilities come from the same Deity. Consequently, no person can stake a claim to superiority because of the gifts he has. Paul bluntly criticized the Corinthians for having puffed-up attitudes:

> For who regards you as superior? And what do you have that you did not receive? But if you did receive it, why do you boast as if you had not received it? (1 Corinthians 4:7).

Paul's point was that no one should have either a feeling of inferiority or superiority (1 Corinthians 12:15-21). We are members of one another in equality, although we have different functions in the church—and every function is important. Leadership is not a superior function.

When Paul listed the several different functions in the church, the person who leads was put in the middle of the pack:

> . . . if prophecy, according to the proportion of his faith; if service, in his serving; or he who teaches, in his teaching; or he who exhorts, in his exhortation; he who gives, with liberality; *he who leads,* with diligence; he who shows mercy, with cheerfulness (Romans 12:6-8).

> And God has appointed in the church, first apostles, second prophets, third teachers, then miracles, then gifts of healings, helps, *administrations,* various kinds of tongues. All are not apostles, are they? All are not prophets, are they? All are not teachers, are they? All are not workers of miracles, are they? (1 Corinthians 12:28, 29).

Notice that "he who leads" and "administrations" are not given a position of preference in the listings. Even the Greek words which are used do not spotlight any superiority. The Greek for "he who leads" *(proistemi)* means to give compassionate care for someone's needs as well as to lead or manage. The word stresses a servant kind of leader. The Greek word for "administrations" *(kubernesis)* means to steer a ship. It was used to designate a helmsman on a ship and is the word from which our word *government* comes. It describes someone who gives direction.

Any organization needs direction as does a ship. Direction is needed most when the emergencies come. As the storm intensifies, the need for a helmsman increases. However, the one who steers the ship is not the only important person on the ship. All the crew members are important as they carry out their varied functions.

To think that he who leads or administrates is the number-one person is to be thinking culturally, not Biblically. Many leaders did not begin wanting to have a superior attitude, but it gradually overtook them because of the attitudes manifested by those who were under their leadership. It is easy for followers to feel they are inferior and almost push the leaders into making all the decisions. They say, "Let them make all our decisions for us. After all, that is their job. We are blindly to follow."

The Road to Authoritarianism. The failure to fulfill the responsibilities within the context of equality in fellowship has caused devastating departures from New Testament Christianity. There is nothing wrong with tradition. The word literally means "handed down." All of us are products of knowledge and practices which were handed down to us. The gospel of Jesus Christ was handed down by preaching and teaching. That truth was called tradition, and early Christians were commended for hanging on to it:

> Now I praise you because you remember me in everything, and hold firmly to the traditions, just as I delivered them to you (1 Corinthians 11:2).

> So then, brethren, stand firm and hold to the traditions which you were taught, whether by word of mouth or by letter from us (2 Thessalonians 2:15).

> Now we command you, brethren, in the name of our Lord Jesus Christ, that you keep aloof from every brother who leads an unruly life and not according to the tradition which you received from us (2 Thessalonians 3:6).

This tradition was fixed in writing in the New Testament for all generations. If what we mean by being hooked on traditions is that we are sticking with the New Testament—that is fine.

However, the original Christian tradition was gradually changed in history by the rise of leadership to an authoritarian note that God never intended it to have. In an attempt to protect the church from many heresies which threatened her, the ministry of bishops, or elders, began to be viewed as an office that was to be a continuation of the apostolic authority. Whatever the bishops said was considered to be "truth." The changes were not noticed at first because they were so minute. A slightly different tradition was passed from generation to generation, but no one noticed because the bishops were trusted, and few people studied the Bible. It was only after many generations had passed that a person would find major changes when making comparisons with the New Testament. The idea of a "ruling elder" arose during this period of gradual change. We can find a reference to a *leading* elder among the elders as early as A.D. 110 (Epistles of Ignatius); however, it was not widespread that early. But by A.D. 250, Cyprian suggested that it was quite widespread and counseled the church to get back to allowing the whole congregation to have the highest priority in matters of government. He even refused to rule on a question which the church asked him to. In his refusal, he explained: "From the very commencement of my ministry I have resolved to do nothing privately, of my own mind, without your advice, and the consent of the people."

By the third century, a council of elders was formed with a president. The center of government was gradually shifted from the congregation to this small group. Elders began to speak as the *only* authority in the church. Their interpretation of Scriptures was to be followed. They began to issue pronouncements and rules without consulting the congregations. The idea of superiors and subordinates arose. Gradually, each bishop (elder) began to control the ministry of all congregations in his area. These bishops even decided who should be ordained.

Thus, what was handed down as tradition from these bishops began to be far different from the original tradition of the New Testament. Finally, the church accepted the concept that one man, the Pope, could establish traditions that were equal to the New Testament. The Pope then became the lawgiver for the church. He began to administrate the worldwide church from a centralized government and treated the church as a corporation. The church became more interested in economy and in its chain-of-command. And all this began when the elders shifted from being leaders equal *with* the members to being leaders superior *over* the members.

While Christians in a free church may declare that having a global church with a central government "could never happen to us," the same type of authoritarianism can happen in each local church. It is possible for a local congregation to have a "ruling elder." If one man has the final veto power on policies and practices of the church, then that church has its own "Vatican City." It is possible for a congregation to be restricted from functioning as the New Testament allows because of its own constitution and bylaws. Every congregation should study carefully its own "law" and evaluate whether it is superceding the New Testament in the life of the church. It is possible for an official board to make all the congregational decisions apart from any consensus of the body. The board meetings may be "closed" and deal with only matters of economy, property, and practices rather than with the development of people in their various ministries. If every minute detail of the business of the church has to be approved by a board, the congregation has its own "ecclesiastical council" that runs the "corporation" church.

When any of the above situations is prevalent, new traditions can be adopted which could gradually (though not noticeably at first) depart from the original traditions of the New Testament. The end result is a congregation that has drifted far from the concept of a New Testament church. Any time authority is turned into authoritarianism, a departure from the New Testament and God's way is certain. In seeking to guide the church today, we must guard against the evils of authoritarianism and meditate upon the concept of the authority of Jesus, the apostles, and the Word of God and determine to fulfill that delegated authority in all humility and love.

CHAPTER TWO

THE DIMENSIONS OF THE CHURCH

God has always used people to develop people. The inspired proverb is still relevant, "Iron sharpens iron, so one man sharpens another" (Proverbs 27:17). If having a Bible eliminated the need for people's leading people, we would not read the following verses within it:

Remember those who **led** you . . . (Hebrews 13:7).

Obey your **leaders** . . . (Hebrews 13:17).

Greet all of your **leaders** . . . (Hebrews 13:24).

Now I urge you, brethren (you know the household of Stephanas, that they were the firstfruits of Achaia, and that they have devoted themselves for ministry to the saints), that you also be in subjection to such men and to everyone who helps in the work and labors (1 Corinthians 16:15, 16).

And the things which you have heard from me in the presence of many witnesses, these entrust to faithful men, who will be able to teach others also (2 Timothy 2:2).

But not so with you, but let him who is the greatest among you become as the youngest, and the **leader** as the servant (Luke 22:26).

Then it seemed good to the apostles and the elders, with the whole church, to choose men from among them to send to Antioch with Paul and Barnabas—Judas called Barsabbas, and Silas, **leading** men *(literally men leaders)* among the brethren (Acts 15:22).

31

And when they had appointed **elders** for them in every church
. . . (Acts 14:23).

God has always provided leaders for His people, because He
knows our needs when we work together as a group. We need
human leaders because of the nature of individuals and the
nature of the church as a whole.

NATURE OF INDIVIDUALS

The first words about an individual came from God, who said,
"It is not good for the man to be alone; I will make him a helper
suitable for him" (Genesis 2:18). The remarkable thing about
that man's situation was that he was daily in the presence of
God. God could and did speak to him directly. That would
certainly be better than having a Bible to read! But God knew
that His presence was not enough for the man; he needed
another human being for fellowship—not because God was
not sufficient, but because God created him to need others.

Nowhere do we see this dependence among humans more
clearly demonstrated than in the birth and development of a
human baby. While some newborn animals can survive without a parent, a human baby cannot survive without either a
parent or a parent substitute. The baby develops mostly by
imitation. He learns to talk by listening to others talk. He learns
how to act and react by watching others. He develops self-
esteem by being loved by others.

We never outgrow this need for others. The proverb says,
"He who separates himself seeks his own desire, he quarrels
against all sound wisdom" (Proverbs 18:1). A person who
thinks he does not need others does not understand his own
natural make-up. God compares us to sheep who are followers
and who will always find a leader, for that is their need as it is
ours. People need people, and that fact does not change when
a person becomes the member of a church or carries a Bible in
his hand.

NATURE OF THE CHURCH

It is true that the Holy Spirit lives in each Christian (1 Corinthians 6:19, 20; Ephesians 2:21, 22). It is also true that the Holy Spirit gives to each Christian gifts of abilities and functions (1 Corinthians 12:4-7; Romans 12:4). But is *not* true that each Christian can then be independent from other Christians and grow spiritually. To think that is to misunderstand the nature of the church.

As a Body. We are baptized into one body (1 Corinthians 12:13), the body of Christ (the church). "And He put all things in subjection under his feet, and gave Him as head over all things to the church, which is His body, the fulness of Him who fills all in all" (Ephesians 1:22, 23). The responsibility of leaders is to present to the Head, Jesus, a healthy body. But when is the body healthy? When is it doing the work of a body?

The work of a body is manyfold: (1) to make the person visible. Just as you cannot see me apart from my body, so people cannot see Christ apart from His body, the church. A congregation which is more interested in people seeing *it* and praising *it* has misunderstood its nature.

(2) To make the person mobile and present. I go where my body takes me, and Jesus is where His body is. He promised, "Where two or three have gathered together in My name, there I am in their midst" (Matthew 18:20). It would be awfully difficult for me to convince my boss that I was at work when my body was home in bed. By the same token, it is awfully difficult to convince the world that Jesus is present when the world aches if the body isolates itself from those hurts.

(3) To reproduce. The physical body is constantly reproducing cells, and so should the body of Christ. God's purpose from before the foundation of the world has been and still is "to bring all things in heaven and on earth together under one head, even Christ" (Ephesians 1:10, NIV). All comes together under one head as the church reaches out to invite and include everyone in the body of Christ.

(4) To do the bidding of the head. Every member in the body is to coordinate and cooperate with the head, Jesus. That means that the body is to be aglow with the attitudes, interests, and activities of Jesus. That is a tall order, for He is God. His attitudes are godly, His interests are varied, and His activities

are as broad as the needs of the people. This is not an impossible task for the church, however; for God has gifted the church with the Holy Spirit so our attitudes can be godly. He has gifted the church with members who have many different interests and abilities. When these are all put together and allowed to function, the church is free to express Jesus' many interests and activities.

One of the greatest setbacks in the church is the tendency for some leaders to paralyze the church by trying to make all the members alike. In doing that, they present to Jesus "clones," not a body in which many different cells function in a variety of ways and yet are united. Paul spotlighted the diversity of individual members within the unity of the body (Romans 12:4-8; 1 Corinthians 12:12-31). In the body of Christ, no one is to have an inferiority complex because he does not function as spectacularly as someone else (1 Corinthians 12:20), and no one is to have an attitude of superiority (1 Corinthians 12:21-26). Leaders must free the individual members to use their God-given abilities in ministry. Then and only then can the total work of God be done on earth. It is to misunderstand the nature of the church to reduce its function to one primary activity such as evangelism or education. Jesus was involved in all sorts of ministries, and the church should be, also. In fact, God gave leaders to the church so they could help equip the members to minister with their various abilities (Ephesians 4:11-15).

Because Christians are fellow members in the same body, each member has the responsibility to look after every other member. Paul wrote, "Each member belongs to all the others" (Romans 12:5, NIV). Why? ". . . so that there should be no division in the body, but that its parts should have equal concern for each other. If one part suffers, every part suffers with it; if one part is honored, every part rejoices with it" (1 Corinthians 12:25, 26, NIV). No Christian is baptized into independence, but into interdependence. No Christian has the right to do his own thing for himself and by himself. While it is true that each Christian is connected to the Head, Jesus, it is not true that Jesus is all a Christian needs. A Christian needs other

Christians. In fact, a Christian cannot make it in this world without the support he gets from other Christians. That is the reason Paul wrote that a Christian is "held together by every supporting ligament" (Ephesians 4:16, NIV). As joints in a physical body are held together by ligaments and need those ligaments to function, so is a Christian connected to other Christians. Part of the function of the leaders is to help individual Christians relate to one another in love and fellowship.

Many people have reduced the organization of the church to *only* this "body concept." They stress that the church is an organism as is a body; it is not an organization. Consequently, the church has just one head—and that is true. But the breakdown comes when they go a step further to declare that the divine Head, Jesus, is *all* the leadership the church needs; the church needs no human leaders. Since each person is a cell in the body of Christ with his own gifts, then he should be totally free to do whatever he thinks the Spirit leads him to do. No organization is needed. The only leaders are those who present to the Head a healthy body as each part does his own thing. It is true that leaders must present to the Head a healthy body; however, that calls for more than just releasing the members to "do their own things." If every Christian is to be totally independent from any human leader, then why have a "body" at all? Instead of having a community, each individual could become a little autonomy within himself. Why, then would the Scripture include such commands as, "Submit to one another" (Ephesians 5:21, NIV)?

There is only one head for the human body, but that head has many subleaders through whom the desires of the head are expressed. The parts of our physical bodies are not connected to the head *only*, but also to other parts of the body that "lead" fellow parts to act and react. Cut off some of those surrounding "leader" cells, and the desires of the head will never get through.

Paul did not accept the idea that since every Christian is an equal member in the body, we have no need for human leaders. In fact, it is in the midst of one of his discussions about the body-life that he spotlighted the fact that God gives some members in the body the gift of leadership (Romans 12:8). The Greek word for "lead" (in Romans 12:8) literally means someone who stands out in front of others. It was used to refer to people who were managers with authority as well as people who showed compassionate care. Paul used it to talk about a father's role in his family (1 Timothy 3:5). This brings us to a second image of the church which also illustrates for us the need for human leaders.

As a Family. The church is called the household of God (Ephesians 2:19). People come into the church through a new birth process. That means we start our Christian pilgrimage as babies in Christ, regardless of our chronological age. As babies, we are to grow up (1 Peter 2:2), and our goal is Christlikeness!

> But speaking the truth in love, we are to grow up in all aspects into Him, who is the head, even Christ (Ephesians 4:15).

> But we all, with unveiled face beholding as in a mirror the glory of the Lord, are being transformed into the same image from glory to glory, just as from the Lord, the Spirit (2 Corinthians 3:18).

Just as we need human leaders to guide us and make some decisions for us in our human families, so we need human leaders to guide us in God's family. Because some fail to acknowledge that people in God's family are in different stages of growth, they have said there should be no control over the people in the church. "Trust God with people" is the keynote cry. That is the kind of permissiveness we used to hear about in theories of child rearing. Such ideas proved to be a disaster in our national family life and will lead to disastrous results in the church as well.

Many say, "Let the church be run by the consensus of the group." That sounds great to us democracy-minded people, but it just does not work. What happens when the majority of the group is made up of newborn babes in Christ? Do we manage our human families like that? We would not allow our newborn infants to make the rules in our household, nor would we allow a toddler to make all the decisions if we wanted a harmonious family life. God does not want His family to be managed in such a manner either.

If trusting God with people means that the leaders of the church must keep their hands off the members, then Paul would not have written any letters to the churches. The mess in the Corinthian church happened because people were not mature in Christ (1 Corinthians 3:1-3). They were not maturing because each person was "doing his own thing" and being independent from the church leadership (1 Corinthians 1—4; 2 Corinthians 10—13). Each member thought he had already arrived at spiritual maturity just because he was a member of the church and had gifts from God's Spirit. When Paul wrote, "You are already filled, you have already become rich, you have become kings without us" (1 Corinthians 4:8), he was repeating their own evaluation of themselves. But Paul's evaluation was that they were "babes in Christ" (1 Corinthians 3:1).

The worst thing Paul could have done would have been to let them "grow up" without any leadership. Instead, he led them by writing them letters about specific issues and behaviors, by visiting them, and by sending leaders to them. But he did not do these things in order to be in "control" as a dictator. He was helping them mature as a father in a family helps his children to mature:

> And we proclaim Him, admonishing every man and teaching every man with all wisdom, that we may present every man complete in Christ. And for this purpose also I labor, striving according to His power, which mightily works within me (Colossians 1:28, 29).

God made us to need one another, to follow, and to lead at times. He intends for us to mature in Christ by being an active member in Christ's body and God's family, which means we are to submit as followers and at times to serve as leaders who are concerned about the spiritual maturity of all the members.

THE GOVERNMENT OF THE CHURCH

Jesus did not promise to build a corporation, but He did

38

promise to build His church. No apostle wrote an inspired epistle to the president of a corporation, but to the people of the church. No corporation has been called the Bride of Christ, the Body of Christ, the Flock of God, the Temple of God, or the Family of God. Only the church has these names. Consequently, the government of the church should not be a duplication of the mangement of a corporation, even if it is the most successful corporation around. The church must adopt God's governmental principles, not man's.

The church must not be tempted by the seemingly successful ways of the world. Jesus refused to be lured into such a mentality when the devil bombarded Him with the methods of human success (Matthew 4:1-11). The church must not adopt principles of the world just because they seem to be working in the world, for she is developing an eternal product—not a time-bound product.

This does not mean the church is not to be interested in bigness. God is certainly interested in bigness. Consider the world He created and how His love spreads to all the creatures in that world. He has commissioned His followers to evangelize all—to disciple the *whole* world. He wants to see all things in heaven and on earth united to Him. And, of course, we know heaven will be big, for it will contain a multitude that no one can count (Revelation 7:9). As long as there is still one person outside the church, the church will not be too big. A church in a city will not be too big even if it has included every person in that city.

However, the concern for bigness does not give us the option to bypass rightness. We must also be concerned about submission to God's will and trust that God knows better than we do how the church can grow to become big and right.

Longevity. Only the church has existed for nearly two thousand years in spite of such obstacles as wars, persecution, economical downturns, and high interest rates. The church survived the stock market crash while many corporations did not. The church has survived significant shifts in industrial interests while many corporations have not. The church has survived the energy crisis while many corporations have not.

One problem with "corporation mentality" is that it fails to plan for longevity. Recently, Dr. Curtis P. McLaughlin, professor of business administration at North Carolina University, observed that American business schools have taught practices which emphasize short-run goals, which eventually result in a decline in industrial productivity. McLaughlin was calling for a different emphasis to be taught. He observed that, too often, business plans and practices are not adopted because they do not lend themselves to *immediate* growth. There is more concern for immediacy than a commitment to the overall good of the company for the years to come. He predicted that the planning process of the business of the future will have to be with the longer range in view and with different growth expectations.

McLaughlin has expressed some of the thinking that has helped the church survive all kinds of cultural changes. The church has been willing to stand up for principles and practices that may appear to hinder immediate growth, but actually enhance growth and longevity. The church has kept a long range perspective with a global outlook. The church got that outlook from Jesus, who could watch a crowd dwindle from twelve thousand to twelve (John 6:60, 66, 67) because He would not compromise His right principles and purposes. Jesus was not interested in short-term, flash-in-the-pan success. He looked ahead to the future and to eternity. Such a perspective is damaged, however, when church leaders start thinking and acting like coroporate executives with only short-range goals in mind.

If we intend to build and run the church like a corporation, we must expect it eventually to collapse. From the measuring stick of eternity, every corporation is a very short-term activity. The following poem, cited by Sam Stone (p. 157, *The Christian Minister*, Standard, 1980), might be amusing until we consider the sad application:

> Like a corporation works the Church of God.
> Brothers, we are treading where Henry Ford has trod.
> We are all mass-minded, one huge body we,
> planning world salvation through the hierarchy.

People-Oriented. The *Wall Street Journal* recently carried an editorial by Jack Falvey, a managing director from New Hampshire. His article was entitled, "The Benefits of Working with the Best Workers," and stressed the importance of managers' working with the most productive workers to get even more out of them. He suggested listening to them, compensating them well, and giving them high recognition and visibility. Then, he says, the management should spend no time with the low producers. Although they might scream for attention, they should receive none unless they are contributing; they should be ignored.

The difference between that corporation mentality and what should be the church's mentality is tremendous. One is interested in using people for productivity; the other is interested in people. Period. If Jesus had followed the philosophy of Mr. Falvey, He would not have spent much time with the twelve apostles. The body-life concept of the church does not permit us to put a higher premium on the more productive parts of the body and ignore the others (1 Corinthians 12:12-31).

The greatest wealth of wasted resources does not lie under the ground in oil, mineral, or other deposits, but above the ground in the earth's most valuable asset—people. Every person is unique with his own set of aptitudes, interests, and creativity. Our own sets of fingerprints are evidence of the matchless distinctiveness of each individual. The major secret of productivity in any endeavor is to tap the wealth of ideas that is locked up inside each person. A church (or any organization for that matter) that does not take that resource seriously is wasting many valuable benefits.

To be developers of programs while neglecting people is a mark of stupidity. The secular corporation has an excuse, but the church with the revelation of God does not have any excuse for such an emphasis. The philosophy of having people-managers must give way to the practice of having people-motivators. People are motivated when they feel they are being treated like people with both abilities and brains to use those abilities. A rigid chain-of-command concept that keeps the little person in his place will fail to draw from that person his finest contributions. One person, or the few who happen to be at the top of the administrative ladder, cannot possibly have as many helpful ideas as those that are stored in the mental savings accounts of people—the members—the common, ordinary people.

Before we pat ourselves on the back and stand assured that we do not treat anyone as superior or inferior in the church, we ought to look at some of our practices. Do we allow a retarded person to greet at the door of the church building on Sunday morning? Do we involve a physically handicapped person, a divorcee, an indigent person, a woman, or a Negro in the work of the church? Is the custodian given any public recognition? Or do we have an unofficial hierarchy that ignores about as many people as it uses? Do we keep people in their places?

A Family Atmosphere. If we want to see unparalleled long-range growth in the church, we need the maturity that sees people "under us" not as subordinates, but as fellow workers. Each person in the church needs to feel the attitude that is summarized in the following: "Do nothing from selfishness or empty conceit, but with humility of mind let each of you regard one another as more important than himself; do not merely look out for your own personal interests, but also for the interests of others" (Philippians 2:3, 4). The idea of a corporation must give way to the idea of a family that treats people with mutual trust and respect. The rigid chain-of-command must give way to the flow of communication that encourages people to participate with creativity.

Communication in the church needs to be so open that people feel they are a part of the process of decision making without being the decision makers. Discontent will then give way to better unity, cooperation, and coordination. Without communication among the whole church family, it becomes easy for one department or subgroup of people to become somewhat isolated from the total church family. Instead of complementation, competition results. Soon, groups of people have no idea what other groups in the church are doing. When decisions are made, it may seem that they are being made "by decree." Such isolation and lack of communication restricts the input the group gets from other spiritually mature members. As this isolation continues, the group will increasingly turn inward, major in only their own interests and be unconcerned about the *whole* of the church, and tend to turn defensive and feel threatened by others who may not have their interests or do not agree with them.

Isolation is fostered by lack of communication. Then, isolation fosters individualism rather than a community spirit. Isolation fosters suspicion, which fosters schisms. Schisms foster defensive mechanisms, which continue to enhance individualism—and the problems within the church increase. The sword of the Spirit becomes the spirit of the sword. Instead of saying, "We do not war according to the flesh" (2 Corinthians 10:3), we declare, "We have the fleshly warfare and armor mastered. No one can outfight us."

If each of us in the church understood what everyone else was doing, we would love and appreciate each other better— as the Scripture says:

> The goal of our instruction is love from a pure heart and a good conscience and a sincere faith (1 Timothy 1:5).

> By this all men will know that you are My disciples, if you have love for one another (John 13:35).

> Owe nothing to anyone except to love one another; for he who loves his neighbor has fulfilled the law (Romans 13:8).

We in the church must realize that spirituality is more important than instant success, service is more important than status, people are more important than projects, following the Lord is more important than climbing ladders, individuals are more important than crowds, and fellowship is more important than enterprise.

CHAPTER THREE

THE MODEL FOR LEADERSHIP

To govern the church, God uses leaders. But when you think about a leader, what characteristics come to your mind? When you think of the bosses you have had, what descriptions rise to your lips? How do you think those who are "in charge" are viewed by the "subordinates"? I have asked these questions of several groups of Christians in the past few years. Their answers are interesting. Here is a partial list:

delegator	ruthless	creative	responsible
decisive	energetic	"big shot"	self-controlled
self-centered	does power-plays	co-worker	puppeteer
example setter	loner	involver	arrogant
administrator	open-minded	flexible	organizer
cold-blooded	servant	human engineer	workaholic
know-it-all	dictator	aloof	manipulator
two-faced	narrow-minded	taskmaster	communicator
trustworthy	dishonest	patient	quick-tempered
peacemaker	gentle	assertive	condescending
insulting	inspector	cooperative	sensible
humble	helpful	unfair	incompetent
unselfish	grouch	competitive	considerate
immoral	stingy	deceitful	understanding

These words describe the primary models that many people observe daily and equate with successful leadership. Many of these models come from the secular world. Consequently, it is easy and almost natural to bring into the church the kind of leadership qualities that we think constitute success in the secular business world. The secular mentality of leadership can creep into the church in at least two different ways: (1) We may purposely look for this type of leaders to hire or elect as our leaders; or (2) When a person is invited to function in leadership role, he may take on his responsibility with the idea that he is to perform as the leaders he has been associated with in the secular world. He may say to himself, "Now I am a leader. I will pattern myself after those leades that I know are successful in the business world."

Whom do you think about when you hear the word *leader?* What names come to your mind? Who do you think is the greatest leader of all time? Some answers that I have received include the following: Hitler, Napoleon, Alexander the Great, Roosevelt, and John Kennedy. If any one of these leaders is a model for us in the church, then it is no wonder the government of the church is in trouble! Hardly ever have I had anyone answer—Jesus. But Jesus' name should have come to our lips first.

I am convinced that no leader has even come close to the stature of Jesus' leadership. Jesus' characteristics of leadership can change any relationship—at home, at school, in the factory, and in business, as well as in the church. For no one knows us better than God. He knows what it takes to lead us properly.

In Jesus, God put on human flesh. Jesus is the image of God (Colossians 1:15), the exact representation of God's nature (Hebrews 1:3), and when we see Him, we see God (John 14:9). Many human leaders have tried to act like a god but totally missed the mark because they did not share the characteristics of the one true God as Jesus did. If any human leader wants to act like a god, then let him become like the real God in attitudes and character. Any official leader in the church should study the life of Jesus closely and have a working knowledge of the leadership qualities of Jesus. How Jesus influenced people is how any Christian leader should seek to influence people in the church.

God equips us to be that kind of leader by giving us the Holy Spirit to work within us. Not only does God equip us, but He also gives us the time and the potentiality to grow up into Christlikeness. When Jesus said, "Follow me," He was not kidding. And we had better not shrug off that invitation. Any church that looks for leaders without first asking how closely the prospects are following Jesus is "barking up the wrong tree." If we shake the wrong tree, the wrong kind of leader will fall into our laps.

Now we could return to the list of characteristics in the first of the chapter and circle those that describe Jesus. All other qualities have no place in leadership in the church. But before we become too smug at our new-found knowledge, let us be sure that those qualities we have circled really describe Jesus. Sometimes our ideas of Jesus do not square with the Jesus presented to us in Matthew, Mark, Luke, and John.

A LOOK AT THE REAL JESUS

Words are always inadequate to sum up Jesus, for He is God's "indescribable gift" (2 Corinthians 9:15). No amount of words can totally capture His essence, but we can see enough of His character to determine whether or not we are becoming like Him or unlike Him in the way we influence people.

1. *Full of grace and truth.* Probably the finest summary of Jesus is in John 1:14: "And the Word became flesh, and dwelt among us, and we beheld His glory, glory as of the only begotten from the Father, full of grace and truth." It is not easy to maintain a balance of grace and truth. Grace involves looking out after another person's well-being, while truth involves doing so in accordance with the absolutes of God. Sometimes we can be full of care, but empty of truthful content. At other times, we can be full of truthful content, but have no kindness. The mature Christian is able to be loving while remaining in the truth (Ephesians 4:15).

2. *Flexible and inflexible.* Jesus' inflexibility is seen in His motivation—to do the will of God, not the will of self (John 6:38). Jesus would not compromise about a "thus saith the Lord." He was inflexible in His moral character.

However, Jesus was quite flexible in His methods. No one was more a slave of God, yet no one was more free. For instance, He varied the way He healed people, the way He taught, the times He prayed, and His activities on the Sabbath.

To follow Jesus correctly, Christian leaders need to be inflexible in the clear commands of God, but allow freedom where there are no commands of God. This dimension of leadership gives us one of our biggest headaches. We like to set up new "laws" in situations where Jesus did not. We tend to judge a person's Christianity by such criteria as how often he worships and by his attendance at mid-week services rather than how often he helps another person. It is one thing to offer opportunities for Christians to participate, but it is another when we elevate those opportunities into legalism.

We can make tremendous progress if we call for conformity in the essentials (clear commands of God), allow liberty in the non-essentials, and demonstrate love in both. When leaders set an example of inflexibility in such matters as the order of the worship service, the time of the service, and who serves at the communion table, they are not using Jesus as their model of leadership. The person who is inflexible is the person who thinks he is infallible.

3. *Lord, yet a servant.* Jesus spoke with authority, but acted as a servant. He was constantly meeting peoples' needs, regardless of the humiliation a lowly kind of service might bring to Him.

4. *The Teacher, yet questioned.* He taught others and knew He was correct in everything He said, but He let the people question what He said without getting upset. He gave people time to assimilate His message and to grow up unto understanding and acceptance. He wanted people to think for themselves and become His disciples out of their own conviction and choice, not because of manipulation or coercion.

5. *Firm, yet gentle.* He never let His opponents control the situation. He was firm with them (remember the woes to the Pharisees), yet He was gentle. In fact, one of the most popular descriptions of Jesus was:

> Behold, My Servant, whom I uphold;
> My chosen one in whom My soul delights.
> I have put My Spirit upon Him;
> He will bring forth justice to the nations.
> He will not cry out or raise His voice,
> Nor make His voice heard in the street.
> A bruised reed He will not break,
> And a dimly burning wick He will not extinguish;
> He will faithfully bring forth justice (Isaiah 42:1-3).

6. *The Overseer, yet the underdog.* He was referred to as the Overseer (1 Peter 2:25, margin) and Chief Shepherd (1 Peter 5:4), yet He was willing to be trampled on by immature people. While many see that as weakness, it was really power under control. Thus, the "power hammers" that pounded away at Him wore out, while He, as the living "anvil," continues on.

7. *He practiced what He preached.* Jesus was not like the executive who, from his office, gives orders to subordinates. He did not lead others by giving out orders. To understand Jesus' way of leading, stretch a piece of string out on a table. Now push it from behind. How far will it advance? But watch what will happen if you take it by the end and pull it. See the difference? Jesus did not lead by pushing people around. He was out in front. He never remained hidden. He was highly visible as a leader.

How could Jesus be such a great leader when these characteristics are so opposed to what we think is necessary for leaders in our world today? The answer lies in His inner character that equipped Him with the ability to lead people by humble service as well as by absolute truths. His inner character could be summed up in three different Scripture passages (Matthew 5:3-9; 1 Corinthians 13:4-7; Galatians 5:22, 23), and the qualities of His character could be listed as follows: Humble, compassionate, gentle, righteous, merciful, pure in heart, peacemaking, patient, kind, not jealous, not boastful, not arrogant, not unbecoming in behavior, not self-seeking, not easily angered, not taking into account wrongs suffered, not delighting in other people's faults, rejoicing in the truth, protecting others, bearing any burden, trusting people, hoping, enduring pressures, loving, joyful, peaceful, good, faithful, and self-controlled.

One statement that summarizes all the qualities listed above is, "He 'emptied Himself, taking the form of a bond-servant' " (Philippians 2:7). Paul captured the core of Jesus' leadership expression when he who so closely imitated Jesus (1 Corinthians 11:1) announced, "I will most gladly spend and be expended for your souls. If I love you the more, am I to be loved the less?" (2 Corinthians 12:15).

What a powerful model of leadership! One who will not only spend what he has, but allow himself to be spent just because he loves, even if he is not loved in return. And notice that he does not do it because he has to, but because he wants to. It is actually voluntary slavery, yet it is not done in drudgery, but delight. That is the heart of a leader who does not care what he gets out of it for himself. He is just concerned about what he is putting into it for what others can benefit.

Turn your eyes upon Jesus.

THE MISUNDERSTANDINGS

It is easy to imitate the wrong model of leadership. The apostles had been with Jesus for three years, and they still looked in the wrong direction when they were seeking to become leaders.

Jesus and His apostles were enroute to Jerusalem, where Jesus would be crucified. Jesus had already demonstrated His authority when He multiplied the loaves and the fishes, and His servanthood when He fed the hungry (Matthew 15). Jesus had also announced His Messiahship and His servanthood role (Matthew 16). Immediately after that, He experienced the transfiguration, which affirmed His authority. Then He came down off the mountain and demonstrated how to serve others by ministering to a lunatic (Matthew 17). After participating in and observing these events, how could anyone miss what was needed to be a great leader? Yet the apostles missed the vital point and began arguing about who would be the greatest in the kingdom of heaven (Matthew 18:1).

Jesus shattered these status seekers by saying, "Whoever then humbles himself as this child, he is the greatest in the kingdom of heaven" (18:4). They were wanting to be Caesars, and Jesus told them to be children.

Matthew then placed a series of Jesus' teachings together at this point to emphasize what it meant to be as humble as a child: (1) He will not use his authority to cause others to stumble (18:7-9); (2) He will not look down upon others (18:10); (3) He will be willing to climb mountains, ford streams, and camp out in order to find even one lost sheep (18:12); (4) He will be willing to forgive someone who has sinned against him (18:15-

20); (5) He will not keep a record of people's wrongs (18:21-35); (6) He will maintain a right relationship with his mate (19:1-12); (7) He will demonstrate special concern to the neglected (19:13-15); (8) He will use his savings account for benevolence (19:16-22); (9) He will be willing to sacrifice anything for God's service (19:23-30); and (10) He will not be jealous of honors that others receive (20:1-16).

Still, James and John flunked the course in understanding great leadership. They equated greatness with a position of status that makes one to be on some type of symbolic pedestal, a notch above others. Their mother asked that special privileges be granted to them (James and John were the lobbyists behind her request; see Mark 10:35-45). They wanted to become two executive vice-presidents and be able to control others (Matthew 20:21).

Jesus replied, "You do not know what you are asking for" (20:22). They were really asking for service, not status, and did not know it. Jesus clarified His statement by saying,

"You know that the rulers of the Gentiles lord it over them, and their great men exercise authority over them. It is not so among you, but whoever wishes to become great among you shall be your servant, and whoever wishes to be first among you shall be your slave; just as the Son of Man did not come to be served, but to serve, and to give His life a ransom for many" (20:25-28).

In essence, Jesus was saying, "You guys have been looking to the secular model of 'successful' leadership, which is not real leadership at all. If you want leadership, look at me. I do not function as the executive does."

Is it possible that we have adopted too much of the mentality of the big corporation into our churches today? The word *minister* simply means *servant,* but have we elevated him to the role of an executive? The word *pastor* means *shepherd,* but have we elevated him to the position of a boss? Have we become too interested in titles and organizational charts? We must not rationalize away Jesus' explanation of greatness.

On another occasion, the apostles were sitting around the

table eating. They began arguing fiercely about which one of them was the greatest (Luke 22:24). The disciples were not simply passing the time with a friendly discussion; they were serious and loving the fight. The seating arrangement at the table might have sparked the dispute. In the first century, the positions at the table signified the order of priority of each guest. The most important guest would be seated to the immediate right of the host. The second in importance would be seated to the immediate left of the host. The third ranking guest would be seated on the right in the second place and so forth. All who were seated at the table would know who was considered the highest or lowest in the eyes of the host. Evidently, some of the disciples thought they had been seated in the wrong places.

Jesus' startling announcement that one of those sitting at the table would betray Him might also have fueled their anger. They began to discuss who it could be, and all eyes would have automatically turned upon the one who was sitting in the lowest position of honor. He would deny it, and they would all begin rehearsing what they had done for and with Jesus and their consequent value to Him.

Jesus listened to their brag session and their disputing, and then He quieted them with a lesson about greatness:

> "The kings of the Gentiles lord it over them; and those who have authority over them are called 'Benefactors.' But not so with you, but let him who is the greatest among you become as the youngest, and the leader as the servant" (Luke 22:25, 26).

In that day, the leaders of the people liked to be known as great. The emperors would have their images imprinted on coins and have words printed under the images that told how wonderful they were (such as, "Benefactor," "God," and "One who deserves to be adorned"). These leaders wanted praise and demanded it.

But Jesus said His followers were to be in direct contrast with such leaders. He said greatness came wrapped up in the package of being willing to be an insignificant person. A young person was considered to be frivolous and trivial, while the aged were respected and honored as being sensible and wise. Jesus was not telling them to act childishly, but to be eager and willing to accept the petty and seemingly unimportant tasks that were assigned to servants and young people.

Jesus went on to say, "For who is greater, the one who reclines at table, or the one who serves? Is it not the one who reclines at table? But I am among you as the one who serves" (22:27). Jesus refused to identify himself with those guests who sit at the table, are served, and are considered by the world to be "great." Rather, He identified himself with the seemingly insignificant hired help who served the guests and ate by themselves in the back room.

Jesus did not just stop with these words; He immediately demonstrated to His disciples what it meant to be great (John 13:1-17). In those days, the roads that people walked upon to get from one place to another were quite dusty. When it rained, they became muddy. Because of the heat, people did not wear shoes like what we wear, but pieces of leather on the soles of their feet tied with a few straps around the ankles. Therefore, at the door of each house would be a pot of water for feet washing. A considerate host would have his slave wash the feet of the guests by pouring water over their feet and wiping them with a towel. It was a lowly task—the lowliest task of all.

There was no slave in the upper room where Jesus and His disciples had gathered. The disciples knew that their feet should be washed when they took their sandals off at the door, but they were more concerned about where they would sit at the table. One of these men should have volunteered to wash the feet of the others. Jesus may have been waiting for one of them to do so. But not one of them realized the type of service they should be willing to give.

Thus, Jesus rose to wash their feet. Jesus never stood taller than when He stooped to wash their feet and wipe them with the towel. He even washed the feet of the man who would betray Him.

Jesus was not setting up a specific ritual that was to be done by all people in all situations. But Jesus was encouraging a certain attitude to be adopted—the attitude of unselfish service for others, even though it may be undignified or humiliating. He was exemplifying the supreme in great leadership.

THE PATH OF GREAT LEADERSHIP

From Jesus' birth to His death, His path to great leadership remained the same. He followed the route of (a) status, (b) to humbled service, to (c) status, which could be diagrammed in this way:

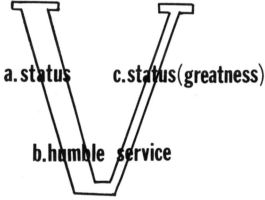

We can ascertain this path in several instances:

(1) John 1:1-14: a. (status) "In the beginning was the Word, and the Word was with God, and the Word was God" (1:1), to b. (humble service) "And the Word became flesh, and dwelt among us . . ." (1:14), to c. (status) "And we beheld His glory, glory as of the only begotten from the Father, full of grace and truth" (1:14).

(2) Philippians 2:6-11: a. (status) "Who, although He existed in the form of God . . ." (2:6), to b. (humble service) "But emptied Himself, taking the form of a bond-servant . . ." (2:7), to c. (status) "Therefore also God highly exalted Him . . ." (2:9).

(3) Matthew 1—28: a. (status) " 'And they shall call His name Immanuel,' which translated means, 'God with us' " (1:23), to b. (humble service) "And Jesus was going about in all Galilee, teaching . . . proclaiming . . . healing . . ." (4:23), to c. (status) "All authority has been given to me in heaven and on earth" (28:18).

The temptation we face is to achieve status without doing humble service. That type of status will never be the greatest in leadership that God desires and demands. Jesus wants all of us to get down in the bottom of the "V." He wants us to become children of God (status), move to humble service by denying ourselves and bearing crosses (Mark 8:34), and know that we will achieve greatness (status, 1 John 3:2).

We cannot hope to be like Jesus in our leadership if we are not serving others. Jesus will not change His philosophy no matter what changes are made in the world around us. Let us determine to become leaders in Jesus' way and achieve true greatness, rather than looking to the model of the secular world and achieve only a worthless and transitory success.

CHAPTER FOUR

LEADERSHIP: PAUL'S STYLE

Can the kind of leadership Jesus modeled be lived out by anyone else? Of course it can, or Jesus would never have said, "Follow me," and Paul would never have written, "Have this attitude in yourselves which was also in Christ Jesus" (Philippians 2:5).

Probably no one lived out Jesus' kind of leadership any better than did Paul. In fact, he wrote, "Be imitators of me, just as I also am of Christ" (1 Corinthians 11:1). He confessed that "For to me, to live is Christ . . ." (Philippians 1:21). We can learn many aspects of leadership from Paul, and we should be sure they characterize our leadership, as well.

1. **He valued truth, not tradition.** No one was more settled into human traditions than was Paul prior to his conversion. He says, "I was advancing in Judaism beyond many of my contemporaries among my countrymen, being more extremely zealous for my ancestral traditions" (Galatians 1:14). It is really tough to walk away from tradition when you have been a leader in those traditions. It is not easy to do and think contrary to one's family upbringing. Yet Paul was willing to make the change. Because he had voted one way in the "board meeting" of his life did not mean he would defend his former position to the end.

One of the worst things church leaders can do is to accept what has happened in past "board meetings" as the primary guide as to what the church can and should do today. Even the bylaws and constitution of the church should not control the church. We must bring the words on those papers underneath the guidance of God's Word.

2. He denied status for service. Few people had more "power" in human status and credentials than Paul. He had accomplished a great deal by putting confidence in the flesh. He liked titles and places of honor (Philippians 3:4-6). His impressive biographical sketch had opened many doors of gain for him, but he admitted, "Whatever things were gain to me; those things I have counted as loss for the sake of Christ" (Philippians 3:7).

The Christian leader is not to get his way because of his position in the community, his titles, his education, his brotherhood recognition, his past accomplishments, or the amount of money he contributes. A person may have given every dime to build a million-dollar building or to buy an organ, but that contribution does not give him the Biblical right to control the use of that building or organ.

Paul was willing to step down from being seen as the "big cheese" to being seen as an insignificant person, as a spectacle, as a fool, as weak, as without honor, as needy, as a common laborer, as the scum of the world (1 Corinthians 4:9-13). The key to Paul's new attitude was that he did not try to make disciples for himself, but for Jesus. In fact, he warned the elders in Ephesus that some from among them would "draw away the disciples after them" (Acts 20:30). To do that is to pervert authority. We must be careful, lest we set up little groups in the church that are more committed to a human head than to the Divine Head—Jesus.

Paul never thought that the church should serve him just because he was an apostle. He was willing to spend and be spent for the church (2 Corinthians 12:15). He was even willing to go to Hell for the Jews if he could (Romans 9:3). He often worked in manual labor as an example to the church members (2 Thessalonians 3:7-9).

Paul's willingness to serve and sacrifice for others is clearly seen in his confession that he did not demand his rights (1 Corinthians 9). Anytime a leader *demands* his rights, he is in serious trouble. Pride has a stranglehold on him.

3. He used authority; he did not abuse it. Paul could have ordered Philemon to receive Onesimus, but he did not. As an apostle, he could have told those gathered at the Jerusalem conference to "like it or lump it," but he didn't. He discussed instead of dictating. He listened as well as spoke (Acts 15).

Paul rightly knew that a man "changed against his will is of the same opinion still." He did not ramrod his view through, even though it was the right view. He knew that many Christians were babes and needed his patience, understanding, and love to help them grow up. He did not come down hard on their imperfections; he manifested grace. Such a reaction allows people time and room to mature spiritually. It instills creativity instead of criticism. The spirit of encouragement, love, and trust motivates people to give their best to the Master, and Paul practiced that spirit. Consequently, he said that God gave him authority to build people up, not to tear them down (2 Corinthians 10:8; 13:10).

Paul could have given the Corinthians an ultimatum to get their house in order or he would give up on them—but he didn't. Instead, he wrote them letters, visited them three times, sent Timothy and Titus to them (separately), and met with Titus later to find out how their problems were turning out (1 Corinthians 4:17; 2 Corinthians 2:4; 2:12, 13; 7:5-16; 13:1). He did nor harangue the people as most bureaucracies do, but he worked as God's leader. He worked *with* people, not *over* them. He knew that leaders could not control the church correctly by ruling her, but must guide her lovingly by serving her.

4. **He considered every member important.** Paul never thought that just the leaders were important. In his writings, there was no such thing as a nobody in Christ's body. He made clear that both feelings of inferiority and superiority would weaken the church (1 Corinthians 12:12-31).

Paul helped a biracial, timid, young person become a mature man of God—Timothy (Acts 16:1, 2; 2 Timothy 1:7). He gave credit to many of his fellow workers (Romans 16). He mentioned some at the beginning of some of his letters (1 Corinthians, 2 Corinthians, Philippians, Colossians, 1 Thessalonians, 2

Thessalonians, Philemon). He protected some of his fellow workers (1 Corinthians 16:10, 11; Philippians 2:25-30). He wrote personal letters to encourage them (1 and 2 Timothy, Titus). He considered every Christian to be a fellow servant (1 Corinthians 3:5-9).

5. He trusted people with responsibility. He knew that one of the best ways to let people mature was to free them to use their abilities and not to fetter them. He sent Titus and Timothy with very significant responsibilities (Philippians 2:19; 1 Corinthians 4:17; 16:10; 1 Timothy 1:3; Titus 1:5).

Church leaders do a tremendous disservice when they think they have to approve every move anybody in the church wants to make. Leaders need to give people room to express their God-given abilities. We need to support people who want to experiment in making their lives count for God.

6. He was flexible. Paul could relate with Jews and with Gentiles without comprosmising his morals or doctrine (1 Corinthians 9:19-23). He said, "For though I am free from all men, I have made myself a slave to all . . ." (verse 19). He recognized the flexibility of the gospel and worked to implement it (verses 22, 23).

7. He was a gentle peacemaker. Paul never carried grudges. Too much leadership energy is drained when we exhibit the spirit of revenge instead of the ministry of reconciliation. Although Paul did not take Mark with him on his second journey, he was not holding a grudge against him, for later Paul wrote, "Pick up Mark and bring him with you, for he is useful to me for service" (2 Timothy 4:11). Paul not only wrote about being a minister of reconciliation, he practiced being one (2 Corinthians 5:16-21).

Further showing Paul's gentleness, he did not harshly criticize or "chew out" the leaders of the churches. When he finished talking with one group of elders, he "knelt down and prayed with them all. And they began to weep aloud and em· braced Paul . . ." (Acts 20:36, 37). It is time every preacher pu aside his criticism of the elders and started praying with them more often, equipping them more adequately, and using them more widely.

8. **He did not use secular approaches.** Paul did not adopt the "how-to-succeed-fast" approaches of his day. Paul himself contrasts his style of leadership with the leadership of the flesh in 2 Corinthians 10—12. It could be charted as follows:

According to the Flesh	Paul's Style
Confidence in externals (2 Corinthians 10:7)	Confidence in Christ-likeness
Putting people down (2 Corinthians 10:8)	Building people up
Terrifying people with words (2 Corinthians 10:9)	Encouraging people with words
Comparing self with self (evaluate accomplishments with the past) (2 Corinthians 10:12)	Making no comparisons
Claiming for self what others have done (2 Corinthians 10:13, 15)	Giving others credit
Preaching another Jesus (watered-down gospel) (2 Corinthians 11:4)	Preaching the true gospel
Depending upon persuasive speech (2 Corinthians 11:6)	Can lead with unimpressive speech
Demanding money that is not due (2 Corinthians 11:7)	Willing to serve without charge
Deceitful, "bait the hook" so people can't see the real thing (2 Corinthians 11:13-15)	Honest
Braging about self (2 Corinthians 11:16-18)	Considering boasting foolish

Enslaving people to self (2 Corinthians 11:20)	Enslaving people to Christ
Taking advantage of people (2 Corinthians 11:20)	Willing to be taken advantage of for service
Seeking people's money and property (2 Corinthians 12:14)	Willing to give up money and property for the people
Authority that makes demands	Service that gives to others

SUMMARY

Paul wrote, "I have been crucified with Christ; and it is no longer I who live, but Christ lives in me; and the life which I now live in the flesh I live by faith in the Son of God, who loved me, and delivered Himself up for me" (Galatians 2:20). This one statement capsulizes the most important perspective a leader must have in order for that leader to have the proper practices. Let us look at Paul's statement closely.

I HAVE BEEN CRUCIFIED: The word "I" is the Greek word *ego*. When Paul was baptized, he buried his ego so he could walk in a newness of life. Every leader must bury his ego, his pride. While discussing the functions of elders, Peter wrote, "Humble yourselves, therefore, under the mighty hand of God, that He may exalt you at the proper time" (1 Peter 5:6). Only then will an elder be leading, not "lording" it over others (1 Peter 5:3).

IT IS NO LONGER I WHO LIVE, BUT CHRIST LIVES IN ME: There is not enough room for both the ego (self) and the Emmanuel to live in one's heart. A person can serve only one master. Every leader must take self off of the throne of his heart and anoint Jesus as the King of his life. Only then does Jesus become the Christ in one's life. How does a leader demonstrate that Christ lives within and not his own ego? By demonstrating the following attitudes and actions:

a. Not thinking more highly of himself than he ought to think (Romans 12:3)
b. Not being conformed to this world (Romans 12:2)
c. Giving preference to one another (Romans 12:10)

d. Contributing to the needs of the saints (Romans 12:13)

e. Not retaliating (Romans 12:14)

f. Not being haughty (Romans 12:16)

g. Accepting those who are weak in the faith (Romans 14:1)

h. Pursuing peace and the building up of one another (Romans 14:19)

i. Pleasing others for their good (Romans 15:1)

j. Not biting and devouring one another (Galatians 5:15)

k. Restoring a fallen brother (Galatians 6:1)

l. Getting rid of revenge and unforgiving attitudes (Ephesians 4:31, 32)

m. Allowing people to have freedom (Galatians 5).

AND THE LIFE I LIVE, I LIVE BY FAITH IN THE SON OF GOD: The leader who trusts Jesus' way and commits himself to that way will adopt the leadership characteristics of Jesus. Faith is not true faith unless it commits oneself to the other person's way. For instance, the Democrats at their National Convention might believe and confess that Ronald Reagan is their president, but they would not be committed to doing things his way. They would believe in Reagan, but they would not have faith in him.

The difference between the devil and a Christian leader is that the devil believes that Jesus is the Son of God but is not committed to adopt Jesus' way of doing things. If a leader only believes in Jesus but is not willing to commit his whole self to Jesus' way, then that leader will act much like the devil, though those ways may be camouflaged.

WHO LOVED ME AND DELIVERED HIMSELF UP FOR ME: This description sums up Paul's kind of leadership as well as that of Jesus. Paul led the church by loving the church and giving himself up for the church.

No leader can lead the people of the church well if he does not do the same—love the church and deliver himself up for her. Let's quit challenging people to become leaders by saying the job is easy and does not require much time, energy, or money. Nothing is further from the truth.

CHAPTER FIVE

LEADERSHIP: BARNABAS' STYLE

A true leader will develop leaders out of his followers. He does not just pull strings on puppets, but he pulls potential out of people. Joseph the Levite was one of the great leaders in the New Testament church because he encouraged people to develop their potentials. His style of leadership won him the nickname "Barnabas," which means *son of encouragement* (Acts 4:36). The word *encourage* comes from a Greek word which literally means to *stand alongside* someone in his need *(paraklesis)*. It spotlights someone who stands by with support, not just a bystander. And Joseph—Barnabas—was just that kind of person.

A real leader stands by people with support and, thus, draws out all kinds of abilities. This characteristic is one of the godly attributes of leadership. Paul wrote that God is the "God of all comfort" (2 Corinthians 1:3). The word "comfort" is the same word as encouragement or support. But God does not comfort, encourage, or support us only to help us when in need, but also to help others *through* us: ". . . who comforts us in all our affliction so that we may be able to comfort those who are in any affliction with the comfort with which we ourselves are comforted by God" (2 Corinthians 1:4).

No person who has not received God's support, comfort, and encouragement can become a true leader in the church. And no true leader can influence people without standing by them with support, comfort, and encouragement. Barnabas loved to spot the potential in people and give them a chance to develop their abilities. He held no prejudices that restricted his encouragement; he encouraged all categories of people, regardless of background, position, or personal style.

THE INDIGENT

Barnabas did not think that poverty was a sign of laziness or that poor people had no potential. He did not adopt a sour sociological explanation for the poor; neither did he ignore them to keep them in their place or hope they would go away. He helped the poor. He sold some of his own property and gave the proceeds to the poor. He did not want to make "charity cases" out of them, but he wanted to show them that he valued them. People who believe they are worth something of value will do actions that are worthy.

It is easy to get discouraged when finances do not go well. No doubt many of the Jewish indigent Christians in Jerusalem had become economically needy because they had become Christians. They were laborers who were fired, businessmen who lost their Jewish customers, and heirs who lost their inheritances because of their commitment to Christ. Barnabas would not let their discouragement overcome them. It is one thing to say, "Cheer up, things could get worse," and, "All things work to the good for those who love God." But is quite another matter to give personal attention to meeting another's needs, to be the instrument God uses to work things for that person's good. Partly because of Barnabas' encouragement, we see in Jerusalem a dynamic church that was willing to remain committed to "the apostles' teaching, and to fellowship, to the breaking of bread and to prayer" (Acts 2:42), and was willing to walk away from everything else for God's cause (Acts 8:1).

A NEWCOMER

The "Hitler of the First Century" was converted and tried to make friends with some Christians in Jerusalem, but he struck out (Acts 9:26). How many new Christians have experienced the same icicle-type reception in the church today? Particularly if they have questionable reputations in the community. Who wants to be seen at the local restaurant with them?

Paul must have been discouraged during those early months of isolation. He, too, wanted to continue not only in the apostles' teaching but also in the fellowship; yet he was not allowed to fellowship with them. I think we can all identify with the reluctance of these Christians. After all, Paul had been the instigator of the persecution in Jerusalem. He had thinned out the ranks of the Christians considerably, and now he was trying to act as a friend to them! They might have thought it was a trick so he could act as a spy. Then Barnabas intervened. He took hold of Paul and introduced him around. Nobody was going to be blackballed in the fellowship as long as Barnabas was on the scene (Acts 9:27).

A true leader will lead the "left outs" as well as those in the "in" group. We would probably be surprised at how many people do not feel a part of the church even after they have been members there for five or ten years. As leaders, we must take special notice of every new member, introduce him around, give him a tour of the facilities, take him to the first few fellowship dinners, and offer any other assistance we are able to give. How many churches have a potential "Paul" who is hiding in the woodwork waiting for a "Barnabas" to help him?

AN INNOVATIVE CHURCH

It does not seem difficult to encourage the church when it is doing what is has always done, but what is a Christian leader to do when the church starts doing something different? The church in Antioch was doing something innovative (Acts 11:19-30). It was the first racially integrated church in Christianity.

Barnabas had been a leader in a segregated church. In fact, some in Barnabas' hometown church had a tough time accepting integration and later criticized the activities at Antioch (Acts 15:1). Yet Barnabas visited this innovative church. He could have said to them, "This is not the way to do it. I've had lots of experience. My home church is very successful. This will never work. No one has ever done it." How often we have seen Christian leaders who have come to a new congregation try to change it into the kind of church they just left! That tendency is repeated constantly in our mobile society. But Barnabas did not approach the situation in that way. He was flexible, not frozen into doing things one way. He did not make up his mind about the church before he got there; he did not condemn or criticize them because they were different. Instead, he saw the grace of God working in that unusual situation (Acts 11:23).

Barnabas encouraged the church at Antioch, and look at what resulted: A congregation that would accept an "outsider" (Acts 11:23); a congregation that evangelized (11:24); a congregation that educated (11:26); a congregation that was said to be Christ-like (11:26); a congregation that was benevolent (11:27-29); a congregation with a team ministry (even the teachers were integrated, 13:1); and a missionary-minded congregation (13:2, 3). The church at Antioch had a balanced program and life. Why? Partly because she was free to develop her potential—because she had a leader who was an encourager. Barnabas did not kill every idea that did not win his instant approval. He realized that a real leader releases people to function for God with their multiple interests and talents.

Many times a congregation may major in only one or two activities because those are the only things the leaders are interested in. People are paralyzed into only those interests. They don't feel free to come up with new programs of upbuilding and outreach. A lopsided emphasis results, and many of the members are not as happy as they might be because they feel there is no place in the church for them to get involved. Let us learn from the example of Barnabas and the congregation at Antioch.

A TRADITIONAL CHURCH

After being a part of a non-traditional church that dares to expand its activities in innovavtive ways, it might be tempting to put down the traditional ways of doing things. But Barnabas was not like that. When the hometown traditional church had need, Barnabas, along with Saul, personally encouraged her (the Jerusalem church) by helping (Acts 11:30).

These leaders knew that God's family was not restricted to any singular locality. A good leader, while caring for his local flock, will also be sensitive to the needs of God's family around the world—even to congregations that may not appreciate his particular congregation (some in the Jerusalem church did not appreciate the congregation at Antioch; Acts 15:1). Perhaps it was Barnabas' example of encouraging a congregation wherever she may be (Antioch or Jerusalem) that helped Paul understand the linkage between the local congregation and the universal church and caused him to write, "To the church of God which is at Corinth, . . . with all who in every place call upon the name of our Lord Jesus Christ, their Lord and ours" (1 Corinthians 1:2).

A FELLOW WORKER

When the congregation in Antioch grew to the extent that another leader was needed, Barnabas looked for one. For whom did he look? Someone right out of Bible college whom he could keep under his thumb? Someone who could not be a possible threat to his own status? Someone who would do all the inconvenient chores? No, Barnabas sought someone who would have the potential to outshine him. He looked for a master teacher and preacher. Why? Because he cared more about the congregation than about himself.

Paul had been in the Tarsus area for several years (Acts 9:30). Most scholars believe that seven to ten years had elapsed since Paul's conversion. Barnabas went to Tarsus to seek out Paul, challenge him with the ministry in Antioch, and encourage him to move there (Acts 11:25, 26).

We can learn an important principle from Barnabas about recruiting leaders. We should not just ask for volunteers. We should go to the person, make eye-to-eye contact, share the vision and the potential, and explain why we think that person should fulfill that responsibility.

A QUITTER

At one time, when Mark was challenged with the reality of mission work, he quit and returned home (Acts 13:13). Thus, Paul did not want to take him on the next journey; but Barnabas saw Mark's potential, knew that he needed help in reaching maturity, and chose to take him along with him (Acts 15:36-40).

Who did the right thing—Paul or Barnabas? Probably both. Paul knew that Mark needed some discipline and gave that. But Barnabas offered the balance of providing an opportunity for further development. Leaders should never lock people into their past mistakes. We must forgive and continue to allow those who may have failed in the past to try again with another opportunity.

SUMMARY

Partly because of Barnabas' encouragement, we have Paul, Mark, and a congregation that sent out men to a global mission. Barnabas led by encouragement and comfort, not by swinging an axe. People followed Barnabas because they wanted to, not because they had to. We should note that Barnabas did not encourage others because he was on the "encouragement committee" of the church. He was not assigned these tasks. He was not merely doing a duty because that was his slot in the hierarchial chain-of-command. He was not hired to be the "encouragement minister." He led in this way because he had this gift; he wanted to lead by helping people.

No one in the church should wait until someone taps him or her on the shoulder and says, "You are a leader now." You might not be on any committee or have any official assignment, but you can still lead out by encouraging and helping others. We all influence somebody. Don't hide under a bushel. There may be a Mark or a Paul who needs you. In fact, we are all exhorted to become like Barnabas by "encouraging one another" (Hebrews 10:25). There is too much in this world to discourage us. Let us not be conformed to this world. Let us lead out in comfort and encouragement.

CHAPTER SIX

GIFTED LEADERS
Part 1

When Jesus departed from the earth, He did not leave the church to run only on its humanity. He gave gifts to people— and still does. "When He ascended on high, He led captive a host of captives, and He gave gifts to men" (Ephesians 4:8). One of these gifts was the gift of leadership. As the Head of the church, Jesus has given her gifted leaders: "And He gave some as apostles, and some as prophets, and some as evangelists, and some as pastors and teachers" (4:11).

This listing is not a hierarchial order, but a chronological one. It lists the leaders in the order in which our Lord gave them to the church: first, the apostles; second, the prophets; third, the evangelists; and fourth, the pastors-teachers.

THE FOUNDATIONAL LEADERS: Apostles and Prophets

The first leaders of the church were the apostles. The word *apostle* literally means *one sent out (apostolos)*. The apostles were those men who were selected and sent out by Jesus him- self. They traveled with Jesus from the baptism of John until the day He ascended. They witnessed His post-resurrection activities (Acts 1:21, 22). They were the first eyewitnesses God used to begin evangelizing the world (Acts 1:8; 2). They were inspired (John 16:13); they were given the ability to do signs and wonders (Acts 2:43); they could confer upon others the power to work miracles through the laying on of their hands (8:14-17; 19:6).

The Lord also called certain persons to be prophets. The word *prophet (prophetes)* literally means *one who speaks before*. It referred to people who spoke about future events (Acts 11:27, 28) and those who preached God's message (Ephesians 3:4, 5). The prophets were directly inspired to continue spreading God's message to the world. Their mission was not only to evangelize, but also to edify, exhort, and comfort the converts (1 Corinthians 14:3, 4). With the absence of written apostolic teaching and with the multiplication of converts, the need for inspired persons was crucial; thus, God provided them (1 Corinthians 12:10; 12:28; 14:29-33).

Both the apostles and prophets spoke inspired messages that became the foundation upon which the church was to build throughout all generations:

> So then you are no longer strangers and aliens, but you are fellow citizens with the saints, and are of God's household, having been built upon the foundation of the apostles and prophets, Christ Jesus Himself being the corner stone (Ephesians 2:19, 20).

These foundational leaders were temporary, for the foundation is laid only once. We do not keep laying a new foundation with a new message from a new apostle or prophet today. However, the church needed leaders when these foundational ones could not be present and after they died; thus, God provided other leaders.

PERPETUAL LEADERS: Evangelists

The work of the evangelist was the first permanent function in the church. Evangelists pre-dated the pastors-teachers. The evangelists started the congregations and often remained with them until the pastors-teachers were developed, but the evangelist did not have to move on when pastors-teachers began functioning. The word *evangelist (euaggelistes)* literally means *an agent of good news* and refers to those who proclaim the glad tidings (a preacher). The activity of an evangelist is described in Romans 10:15: "How beautiful are the feet of those who bring glad tidings of good things!"

While all the apostles and prophets functioned as evangelists, not all evangelists were apostles or prophets. Not all evangelists were divinely inspired (2 Timothy 2:2). However, the evangelists continued the preaching ministry of the apostles by basing their message upon the foundation that the apostles and prophets had laid.

Besides the designation in Ephesians 4, the term evangelist is used only two other times in the New Testament: to refer to Philip and to Timothy. The evangelist may be engaged in a missionary-kind of activity as was Philip when he went to Samaria and when he converted the Ethiopian Eunuch (Acts 8:4-37). Philip also traveled to other cities (Acts 8:40). Evidently when Philip reached Caesarea, he remained there. Several years later, Paul stayed with Philip, who was living in Caesarea and was called an evangelist (Acts 21:8). Paul called Timothy an evangelist while Timothy was in a settled congregation (2 Timothy 4:5).

The good tidings that an evangelist shares involves both preaching to the lost and edifying the saved. The gospel does not only begin a congregation; it also builds it up (Colossians 1:5-8; 1 Corinthians 15:1). Jesus gave the church evangelists partly to equip the saints until maturity is reached (Ephesians 4:11, 12). Consequently, we know that New Testament evangelists did not have to stay on the road to qualify as evangelists.

Recruiting Evangelists. While the apostles received their commission directly from Jesus, evangelists sometimes received their commission from the churches. While Philip received instructions from the Lord to meet the eunuch (Acts 8:26-29), the elders of a congregation set Timothy apart to his responsibilities (1 Timothy 4:14). Although Jesus gave certain people this gift, the evangelist is still the servant of the church.

It is the responsibility of the church to look for potential evangelists. The church today may be too hasty in setting apart anyone to the preaching ministry just because that person has announced his intentions to preach. Recruitment of evangelists should not be the task of Bible colleges and seminaries. Their task is to *help train* evangelists. However, the recruitment and *first* training of the evangelists should come from the churches, just as it was for Timothy and Philip.

Our churches would do well to follow Paul's example in spotting a potential evangelist and giving him an opportunity to be an "intern," much as Paul gave to Timothy when he took him with him on his journeys and continued to expose Timothy to the varied functions of an evangelist.

Our preachers should seek out certain people who could fulfill the role of evangelist and should invite them to work with them as they go about their tasks. Prior to sending any student to a Bible college or seminary, why not allow him to be an "intern" at the church for at least six months? During that period, the intern could be exposed to the diversity of responsibilities that are included in the job—such as sermon preparation, preparations for weddings and funerals, evangelistic calling, pastoral calling, and attending elders' meetings. The church could even consider putting the intern on a salary during that time. A preacher's goal should be to have at least one intern working with him most of the time.

Too many times, a person enters Bible college without the slightest idea what the preaching ministry is all about, and he can never really get the "feel" of the job by classroom work. Nowhere can he learn better the practical aspects of the preaching ministry than in the work of a local cogregation. The Bible college and seminary can help sharpen his tools, but the church should recruit, initially train, and ordain evangelists.

It is irresponsible for a congregation either to ordain someone to this ministry whom it does not know well or to lose contact with the man it ordains. To set apart an evangelist is to set him apart to the church *at large*. Every congregation owes it to every other congregation to know that the man it ordains handles both the gospel and his moral life properly. Many congregations ordain anyone who asks and then do not maintain contact with the person; they are not providing any practical service for the edification of the family of God in that way.

The Responsibilities of Evangelists. An evangelist is to be a protector of the gospel (1 Timothy 1:3-5), an example setter (1 Timothy 4:12, 16) 2 Timothy 2:22), a teacher (1 Timothy 4:11), a student (1 Timothy 4:13), and a preacher (2 Timothy 4:2). He should conduct himself properly (1 Timothy 3:15) and be committed to sound doctrine (1 Timothy 4:6, 7; 6:20; 2 Timothy 1:13; 2:14, 15; 3:14). He should relate well to people (1 Timothy 5:1-4) and let the elders function as they should (1

Timothy 5:17). He should take care of himself physically (1 Timothy 4:8; 5:23). He needs to be committed to his work as an evangelist (2 Timothy 2:3-6), be firm, gentle, and not quarrelsome and yet be a corrector of false teaching (2 Timothy 2:23-26). He should recruit other evangelists (2 Timothy 2:2), protect the elders (1 Timothy 5:19, 20), and lead out in disciplinary matters (Titus 3:10, 11).

These stated responsibilities do not exhaust what an evangelist does; neither do they tell *how* a person is to perform these functions. Each person is different, with his own set of abilities, and will handle the job differently than anyone else. He may do much of his teaching through counseling or on a one-to-one basis or through small group meetings rather than in a classroom setting. The congregation should allow the evangelist the freedom to work in those areas and use the methods that best suit him. We do not take seriously the diversity of God's gifts when we insist that the evangelist be just like the former one or fit into our mold.

It would not be wise to invite an evangelist to function in a congregation and then not trust him to function. When he has to have approval for every move he makes, he is not free to function as he could and should. Some evangelists cannot invite a speaker or a musical group, or attend a conference, without permission. That hardly expresses the mutual trust that mature members in God's family should have with one another. Just as the children in our human families gain more freedom as they mature, so it should be in the family of God. If a man is mature enough to be an evangelist, he should have the freedom to act as one. At the same time, the evangelist should not take advantage of the freedom he has and start dictating what he will do with no regard for anyone else. Trust should extend both ways.

The church in Antioch trusted Barnabas enough to allow him the freedom to choose his own associate (Acts 11:25, 26). Paul trusted Timothy enough to leave him in troubled churches (1 Timothy 1:3). He trusted Titus enough to put him in charge of appointing elders (Titus 1:5).

Paying the Evangelist. Some preachers feel guilty when they receive a paycheck, but they should not. Paul made it clear that the Lord directed those who proclaim the gospel to get their living from the gospel (1 Corinthians 9:14). At times, Paul made tents to earn money, but that was not his normal method for receiving income. While alone in Corinth, he made tents; but that restricted his evangelistic efforts to just one day a week (Acts 18:1-4). When his associates arrived, he began "devoting himself completely to the word" (18:5). Why the difference? Because his associates brought funds from other churches (Philippians 4:15, 16; 2 Corinthians 11:7, 8); thus, he did have to rely on working on tents for his living while he worked with the young church there.

When Paul worked in Thessalonica, he did not do it only to receive income, for he received money from the Philippian congregation (Philippians 4:15); but he worked to be an example to the congregation, whose members tended to be lazy (2 Thessalonians 3:7-12).

Jesus called His twelve apostles away from their usual line of work, but He did not expect them to draw from their own financial resources to continue working for Him. While they preached, others provided their needs (Luke 8:1-3). When Jesus sent them out, He did not expect them to take their own resources; He said the people would provide for them (Matthew 10:8-15).

It is a ministry for the body of Christ to free one or more people from other responsibilities so he or they can be available to meet the pressing needs of the congregation. Hiring a preacher should be seen as performing a service with the people. It is in effect saying, "We are freeing you from plowing the fields, working on the assembly line, selling products, or running an industrial office to share the Word with our congregation in what you say and in what you do."

Our complex, fast-moving society makes such a specialist necessary. Before endeavoring a full-time ministry, I was a control tower operator at O'Hare Airport in Chicago. I worked six days a week because fully qualified operators were low in number. I was totally free on only five Sundays a year. I worked in shifts; every five weeks my day off changed. Every man in the church I attended at the time was in a similar situation. The body of Christ there needed a full-time worker to meet the needs, for no one else was available.

Freeing a man from "tent-making," so to speak, calls for financial remuneration. The Lord did not expect people to refrain from work and then not receive financial help—and neither should we. But paying the preacher does not let the rest of us members off the hook. The church's problems are not caused by our having paid servants in the church, but they may be related to how these people use their time. Do the full-time workers do *all* the work of the church? That is not Biblical. Or do they equip and allow the members to help? That is Biblical. Every member is to be a minister. We all have some kind of service to contribute, no matter what our schedule. All of us work together to expand and mature the church.

None of us can hire a preacher and expect him to study for us. We must study God's Word, also. None of us can expect the preacher to pray for us; we must pray. None of us can expect the preacher to witness for us. We all have opportunities to testify and must use them. We cannot expect the preacher to do all the preaching. Paul was not the only preacher on his team; he equipped others to preach and allowed them to. The church in Antioch used several preachers (Acts 13:1). Our preachers should invest some of their time in equipping others to preach.

None of us can expect the preacher to take our place in the nursing home or on hospital visits; we must be visiting there, too. But we can expect the preacher to be available and be present at times when we cannot. We can expect him to devote himself fully to the Word because we cannot. This does not mean we must expect him to work constantly with no time off. He is not our slave. He is our partner and brother in the ministry of Christ. To employ a paid preacher is Biblical, but to treat him like a temporary hired hand is not. May our preachers not feel guilty because they are paid, and let us not squabble about salaries.

Relationship Between Evangelists. We can learn much about the relationship between evangelists from studying the relationship of Barnabas and Paul and Paul and Timothy. Some of the lessons may be painful.

When Barnabas and Paul began working together, they were known as "Barnabas and Saul" (Acts 13:2, 7), but soon they were known as "Paul and his companions" (13:13) or "Paul and Barnabas" (13:42). Notice the change in the order of names. Paul started to outshine Barnabas. But Barnabas did not mind one little bit. A real leader is not threatened by another leader. A real leader delights to see God's gifts in another person develop to full potential.

What would happen today in many churches if the popularity and effectiveness of the new "associate" began to surpass the "senior" minister? The new associate may plan for that to happen and pull some strings to make it happen. That would be perverted leadership. Paul was not like that. Or the "senior" minister might be so threatened that he would criticize and undercut the associate. Barnabas was not like that. The mark of humility, one of the basic attitudes of true Christian leadership, is seen in the reactions of both.

A Barnabas-style leader does not get jealous if another person is asked to preach a funeral, play the organ, or sing a solo. A Barnabas-style minister is not threatened when his predecessors come back to town to visit or are asked to perform a wedding. Why is it that we often teach as "ministerial ethics" that once we leave a church, we must stay away? This is not the New Testament concept of fellowship and service. No person has the right to say, "This is my territory. Keep out."

An evangelist makes friends as well as converts. He has a church full of brothers and sisters, not just listeners. Thus, it is not natural to expect that a person cut off all active caring about these people when he moves away. A new evangelist should not be threatened by people who express love for a previous evangelist. He should accept that as positive evidence that the congregation loves its evangelists. At the same time, a new evangelist will find that there will be complaints about his predecessor, but he should make no comment. He can learn about people's needs by their complaints, but he must not take sides.

An evangelist should not become jealous or read rejection into the action when someone requests a former evangelist come to perform a funeral or wedding or baptism. I once followed a preacher who had been at the church for a decade. He had poured himself into the lives of the people. He had participated in their joys and disappointments, their births, sicknesses, deaths, baptisms, and marriages. So when a serious illness hit a family, I asked if they would like for me to let the former minister know. The people were so relieved that I was not threatened by their love for him. I also asked if the church members would like for me to invite him to perform weddings and funerals. At first, they did; but as time wore on, the requests diminished and then stopped. But how much harm would have been done if I had felt threatened and become angry about their feelings for that former evangelist. This way, there were only good feelings to remember.

At the same time, an evangelist who has moved away should not be still guiding the church by remote control. He should not give advice or services without being invited. Evangelists need to apply the golden rule to their relationships to each other as well as all other people.

Paul had every right to keep Timothy under his thumb as his assistant. But he did not. He included Timothy's name when he wrote many letters and called himself Timothy's father (1 Corinthians 4:17)—a term of love, not a putdown. He called Timothy a fellow worker (1 Corinthians 16:10) and a brother (2 Corinthians 1:1). He bragged about him (1 Corinthians 16:10; Philippians 2:19-22); he protected him (Acts 16:3). He equipped Timothy and delegated important tasks to him. Paul gave him credit (2 Corinthians 1:19). Paul wrote Timothy letters of encouragement (1, 2 Timothy) and longed to see him in the final period of Paul's life (2 Timothy 4:9).

As the younger associate, Timothy never tried to get the limelight away from Paul. He never tried to "take over." In fact, he knew how to take orders and carry them out. There was mutual respect, trust, and love between the two. Cooperation and coordination did not allow room for competition. Every team ministry needs to duplicate that of Paul and Timothy.

78

The Position of Evangelist. Although the preacher is not to be
seen as just a temporary hired hand, he is not to see himself as
superior to others either. He is not the boss. Although he may
teach potential elders and help develop them to function as
elders, he is not the overseer of the elders. He is not the
pastor, although he may do pastoral functions. The elders are
the pastors of the church. The preacher may be one of these if
he is so elected, but he is not one automatically.

But at the same time, we must realize that the preacher is to
be a leader. We are to allow him to be a man of God who can
lead and guide us. God has consistently used one person to be
the motivating and goal-setting leader for people. Men like
Moses, Joshua, David, Ezra, Solomon, Nehemiah, and Paul
would have melted into mediocrity had the people seen them
as hired hands instead of leaders. However, none of these men
functioned in isolation from others, but used the counsel of
others. They worked with other leaders, such as the elders. Yet
they were the "out front" men, giving direction without being
dictators.

A congregation that will not allow someone to be a visionary,
motivating, and creative leader will not advance very far. There
has been a tendency to sit on potential leaders for fear they will
become dictators. That is a danger with any leader, but it does
not give us the mandate to remain neutral and go nowhere.
Fear of the negative can paralyze us. Why not maintain faith in
the positive? Why not let a person be our "spark"? We all need
to be stretched, and we need a person in front of us challenging us with possibilities. Freeing a person to do that can further
free the elders to shepherd the flock, which will be continually
growing and serving.

We need one another in the church. Let us be a family and
treat one another and our leaders with respect. Let us be a
body and work together in harmony toward the goals our leaders set before us.

CHAPTER SEVEN

GIFTED LEADERS
Part 2

PERPETUAL LEADERS: Pastors-Teachers

Another category of leaders that were to be leading perpetually in the church were the "pastors and teachers" (Ephesians 4:11). Although pastors and teachers can be two different people, in this verse in Ephesians 4, the Greek construction refers to the functions of one person. In other places, however, teachers are listed as having a function apart from the function of pastors (Acts 13:1; Romans 12:7; 1 Corinthians 12:28). So why were the two functions linked together so closely in the Ephesians passage? Because the thrust of the meaning in that verse is that all pastors are also teachers.

The Greek word for *pastor (poimen)* means *a shepherd*. This word is used seventeen times in the New Testament and refers to the following: (1) Keepers of sheep (Matthew 9:36; 25:32; Mark 6:34; Luke 2:8, 15, 18, 20; John 10:2); (2) Jesus (Matthew 26:31; Mark 14:27; John 10:11, 14, 16; Hebrews 13:20; 1 Peter 2:25); (3) Leaders of the church (Ephesians 4:11). These leaders of the church (pastors) are the elders, who have been given the responsibility of shepherding:

> Be on guard for yourselves and for all the flock, among which the Holy Spirit has made you overseers, to shepherd the church of God which He purchased with His own blood (Acts 20:28).

> Therefore, I exhort the elders among you, as your fellow-elder and witness of the sufferings of Christ, and a partaker also of the glory that is to be revealed, shepherd the flock of God among you . . . (1 Peter 5:1, 2).

Biblical terms for Elders. Two other Greek words that refer to an elder (besides *poimen)* are very important to understand. The first is *presbuteros* (from which the word presbyterian comes). It literally means *an older person* and is used sixty-six times in the New Testament in four different ways: (1) An older person (Luke 15:25; Acts 2:17); (2) Leaders in Judaism (Matthew 16:21; Acts 4:5); (3) Leaders in the church (Acts 11:30; 14:23); (4) A representative group of worshipers in Heaven (Revelation 4:4; 5:5). When this word refers to a leader in the church, it is translated into English by the word *elder*. Thus, every time you see the word *elder* in your English text, *presbuteros* is the Greek word behind it.

The second word referring to elders is *episkopos,* which is used only five times in the New Testament in two different ways: (1) Jesus (1 Peter 2:25); and (2) A leader in the church (Acts 20:28; Philippians 1:1; 1 Timothy 3:2; Titus 1:7). The main part of the word—*skopos*—is the word from which we get our English word *scope* and literally means to *look or see.* The prefix *epi* means *over or upon.* Thus, the word means *overseer.* This word translated into the English becomes *bishop, overseer,* or *guardian.*

Since both of these Greek terms are used interchangeably, we can conlude that they refer to the same leader, as they do in Acts 20:17-38; 1 Timothy, and Titus. In Acts 20:17, Paul called to him the elders of the church *(presbuteros).* As he talked to them, he referred to them as being made by the Holy Spirit to be overseers *(episkopos,* Acts 20:28). When Paul wrote to Titus about elders, he used the two words interchangeably:

> For this reason I left you in Crete, that you might set in order what remains, and appoint elders *(presbuteros)* in every city. . . . For the overseer *(episkopos)* must be above reproach . . . (Titus 1:5-7).

These words are significant in understanding the task of the elders because one spotlights the maturity of the person (elder, *presbuteros),* while the other stresses his function (overseer, *episkopos).* An elder is to be a mature Christian who oversees the church. Now we must consider what it means to be an overseer.

An Overseer in the New Testament. The English word "overseer" brings all types of images to our minds. We know about overseers in the military, in prisons, in governmental agencies, and in business. Is the overseer in the church to be like the guards that oversee a prison courtyard? Is he to be like a drill sergeant or a five-star general? Is he to be like the inspector or foreman who oversees the assembly line? Is he to be like the big boss through whom every minute decision must get an approval? There are many types of overseers in the world, but are they to serve as our models for overseers in the church?

To answer that question, we should study carefully how the verb form for "overseeing" is used in the New Testament to see what *activity* an overseer in the church should be doing. I think we will find it quite revolutionary when we fully realize what God means by overseeing, for its usage has been hidden by translators who have not translated the word into English as "overseeing." As we look at every verse in which the verb form (*episkeptomai; episkopeo*) is used, I will italicize the word because it is not easy to spot the word in the English. As we do so, we should be asking, "What kind of overseeing is being described?"

1. **Matthew 25:35, 36.** In this text, Jesus was discussing the separation which will take place at the Second Coming. Part of the criteria at the Judgment will be our sensitivity to care for people's needs:

> For I was hungry, and you gave Me something to eat; I was thirsty and you gave Me drink; I was a stranger, and you invited Me in; naked, and you clothed Me; I was sick, and you *visited* Me; I was in prison, and you came to Me.

In the phrase in which the verb "overseeing" appears, Jesus was saying, "I was sick, and you *oversaw* me." But what kind of overseeing was it? Was it an inspection or a judgment that said "we told you so"? Was it a visit that just left a calling card while the person slept? The context is clear. The verb did not mean so much of a "seeing over" as a "looking upon" with care. In fact the *New International Version* correctly translates the verb, "you looked after me." (It is disappointing, however, that the

NIV does not translate the word in this way in other places it is used.)

2. **Matthew 25:43.** In this passage Jesus was showing the opposite of the former passage we considered:

> I was a stranger, and you did not invite Me in; naked, and you did not clothe Me; sick, and in prison, and you did not *visit* Me.

Again it is clear that the verb is not describing the type of overseeing that the guards or wardens of a prison exercise. Those people imprisoned because of their Christianity would need no more guards, but they did need people who would look upon them with care. The *NIV* translates it, "did not look after me." To look upon or to look after someone communicates an entirely different view of an overseer than we usually see in the world.

3. **Luke 1:68.** In this verse, Zacharias, as he was thinking about the coming of the Messiah, was inspired to say, "Blessed be the Lord God of Israel, For He *has visited* us and accomplished redemption for His people." Literally Zacharias was saying, "He has overseen us." What kind of overseeing was it? Jesus *looked after* our needs and was able to accomplish redemption for His people in that way. This overseeing was doing something for people who were in desperate need.

4. **Luke 1:78.** Zacharias continued to speak about the coming of the Messiah: "Because of the tender mercy of our God, With which the Sunrise from on high *shall visit* us." Literally he said, ". . . shall oversee us." This type of overseeing obviously had its source in the mercy of God. As we read the rest of Luke's Gospel, we clearly see that Jesus came to meet people's needs. He came to look after us, not just to look over us. He could have looked over us without coming to earth. But He cared so much about our needs that He died for us.

5. **Luke 7:16.** In this text, Jesus had just interrupted a busy schedule to care for the widow who had lost her only son by death (7:11-13). The funeral procession was in progress when Jesus raised the boy from the dead. The witnesses reacted in this way: "And fear gripped them all, and they began glorifying

God, saying, 'A great prophet has arisen among us!' and, 'God *has visited* His people!' "

They literally said, "God has overseen His people." But what kind of oversight was this? God had taken care of a need. God was looking after His people. The margin of the *New American Standard Bible* translates it, "Cared for."

6. **Acts 6:3.** The church was growing so fast that it was difficult for the apostles to get around to help all the needy widows as well as do their praying, preaching, and teaching. So they gathered the congregation together and said, "But *select* from among you, brethren, seven men of good reputation, full of the Spirit and of wisdom, whom we may put in charge of this task." Literally they said, "Look over or upon you seven men."

7. **Acts 7:23.** Stephen was rehearsing some significant Jewish history when he reminded the audience about Moses, who was raised as an Egyptian while the Hebrew people were enslaved. Moses' upbringing could have caused him to be hardhearted against his own people: "But when he was approaching the age of forty, it entered his mind to *visit* his brethren, the sons of Israel."

The literal translation would be, "It entered his mind to oversee his brethren." What kind of oversight did Moses mean to exercise? Did he want to be another taskmaster? No, they had plenty of them already. Moses wanted to look upon and to take care of his people in their need. In fact, he killed a taskmaster (overseer) who was being cruel to his people. Moses intended to deliver his people from slavery (Acts 7:25).

8. **Acts 15:14.** A dispute had arisen in the church about evangelizing Gentiles without circumcising them. As part of the discussion, James said, "Simon has related how God first *concerned Himself about* taking from among the Gentiles a people for His name." Literally, James said, "God oversaw to take out of the Gentiles. . . ." Here again, God's oversight was *looking after* the Gentile's needs. It was showing a compassionate concern which moved Him to take care of the Gentiles.

9. **Acts 15:36.** "After some days Paul said to Barnabas, 'Let us return and *visit* the brethren in every city in which we pro-

claimed the word of the Lord, and see how they are.' " Literally, Paul said, "Let us return and oversee. . . ." It is clear that Paul wanted to look upon them to see how they were in order to look after their needs.

10. **Hebrews 2:6.** Here the writer is quoting Psalm 8:4: "What is man, that Thou rememberest Him? Or the son of man that Thou *art concerned about* Him?" Literally, the Psalmist said, ". . . that Thou oversaw Him?" The context makes it clear that this oversight is a looking upon to look after man's needs. The overseer (God) takes care of man's deepest needs (Hebrews 2:7, 8).

11. **Hebrews 12:15.** In discussing some practical applications of being in Christ, the writer said, *"See to it* that no one comes short of the grace of God; that no root of bitterness springing up causes trouble, and by it many be defiled." The literal translation is, "Pursue peace (12:14) while *looking after* that no one comes short. . . ." The overseeing here means looking after people's need to protect them from being defiled.

12. **James 1:27.** "This is pure and undefiled religion in the sight of our God and Father, to *visit* orphans and widows in their distress, and to keep oneself unstained by the world." Literally, James was saying that we should "oversee" orphans and widows. But the context makes it obvious that we are to look upon them to look after them in their need.

13. **1 Peter 5:2.** "Shepherd the flock of God among you, *exercising oversight.*"* This kind of oversight is in the context of a shepherd who looks after the needs of the sheep.

After considering the usage of the verb form of overseeing, we can conclude that God's kind of overseer is to look upon the needs of the people for the purpose of looking after them. Thus, the person who oversees the church will be one who looks upon the church with compassionate concern and will take care of the needs of the people.

---

*Only editions of the NASB printed with a 1977 or later copyright have this expression. Other versions, such as NIV and King James, also have it.

An Overseer in the Old Testament. The Greek word for over-seer *(episkopos)* is used in the Old Testament to refer to the responsibility of priests (Numbers 4:16), military captains (Numbers 31:14; 2 Kings 11:15), and supervisors of work (2 Chronicles 34:12; Nehemiah 11:9, 14, 22). We have been much too quick to follow these models in our leadership without due consideration of the rest of the picture. What we have seen from the New Testament and what we will see from the Old Testament must temper this view. Since Jesus is the only per-sonal example elders are exhorted to follow, only the divine model is a valid example, and not these other Old Testament leaders. Thus, we must look to God and see what type of over-seeing He did in the Old Testament. The verb form for oversee-ing is used several times to describe God's looking upon peo-ple to care for their needs. Here are some of these instances:

> Then the Lord *took note of* Sarah . . . so Sarah conceived (Genesis 21:1, 2).

> God *will* surely *take care of* you (Genesis 50:24, 25).

> I *am* indeed *concerned about* you (Exodus 3:16).

> The Lord *was concerned about* the sons of Israel (Exodus 4:31).

> The Lord *had visited* His people in giving them food (Ruth 1:6).

> And the Lord *visited* Hannah; and she conceived (1 Samuel 2:21).

> What is man, that Thou dost take thought of him? And the son of man, that Thou *dost care for* him? (Psalm 8:4).

> Thou *dost visit* the earth, and cause it to overflow; Thou dost greatly enrich it (Psalm 65:9).

> Look down from heaven and see, and *take care of* this vine (Psalm 80:14).

> *Visit* me with Thy salvation (Psalm 106:4).

> *I will visit* you and fulfill my good word to you, to bring you back to this place (Jeremiah 29:10; LXX—Jeremiah 36:10).

> Behold, I Myself will search for My sheep and *seek them out.* As a shepherd cares for his herd, . . . so I will care for My sheep (Ezekiel 34:11, 12).

Notice that each time the verb is used, it describes God's active looking upon for the purpose of looking after the needs of people. There are some possible exceptions to this statement. But a careful consideration of these usages reveals that they also spotlight God's care of His people.

One possible exception deals with God's looking upon His people to discipline them: "Then *I will visit* their transgression with the rod, and their iniquity with stripes" (Psalm 89:32). Yet God's discipline is not to destroy us, but to deliver us from our habitual sinning (Hebrews 12:5-13). Human overseers in the church are also to exercise discipline for the good of the Christians.

The other possible exceptions describe God's looking upon the enemies of His people for the purpose of punishing them (Psalm 59:5; Isaiah 10:12; Jeremiah 5:9, 29; 9:9, 25; 11:22; 27:8; 29:32; 30:20; 44:13; 49:8). This may sound as though God is being a cruel "overseer," but He is not. God punishes for the purpose of getting the enemies of His people to repent and of protecting His own people. God's people do not have to take vengeance on them with their own hands (Romans 12:19-21). Even in this way, God is looking after us with tender protection and care.

The verb "overseeing" also describes activities of God's people, and in each instance, it is the activity of caring: Priests' examining an infectious person (Leviticus 13:36)—the infectious person was quarantined to protect other people—Samson's caring for his wife (Judges 15:1); and David's taking food to his brothers (1 Samuel 17:18). This verb form is also the same verb that is used when referring to the numbering of God's people to use them in service. Even here we can see God's care for His people, as the army was designed to protect God's people and claim His land promises.

SUMMARY

Although the noun "overseer" may cause us to think about the many different types of overseers, we should take our clue of the kind that God had in mind for the church by the way the activity of overseeing is described in the Scriptures. In both Testaments, overseeing is not describing a "looking over" from the position of a superior, but a "looking upon" from the practice of a servant who looks upon in order to discover needs of people so those needs can be looked after. That is the primary function of the elders (pastors-teachers) of the church. They are to see to it that the needs of the people are looked after. The study of the two primary models for the elder will also substantiate this vital function. We will study them in the next chapter.

CHAPTER EIGHT

THE ELDERS
AS SHEPHERDS

Even in the first century, the secular example of leadership was an inappropriate model for the overseer in the church (Matthew 20:25-27). Certainly it is no more appropriate today. The kind of overseer that God wanted for the church was such a new type of leader that examples of it were scarce.

There were basically two models expressed in Scripture—the personal and the professional. Jesus himself was the personal model the church overseers were to imitate: ". . . just as the Son of Man did not come to be served, but to serve, and to give His life a ransom for many" (Matthew 20:28). The apostle Peter saw Jesus as the overseer and called Him that: "For you were continually straying like sheep, but now you have returned to the Shepherd and Guardian *(episkopos)* of your souls" (1 Peter 2:25).

Because Jesus is to be the model for the overseers in the church, we would be wise to choose those men whose attitudes, actions, and reactions most resembled Jesus'. We should ask, "Is this the priority that Jesus would make?" "Is this the way Jesus would act?" "Is this the decision Jesus would make?"

The professional model an overseer is to imitate is the shepherd. Connecting the overseers of the church with shepherding is clearly shown in the New Testament:

> Be on guard for yourselves and for all the flock, among which the Holy Spirit has made you overseers, to shepherd the church of God which he purchased with His own blood (Acts 20:28).

> Therefore, I exhort the elders among you . . . shepherd the flock of God among you . . . (1 Peter 5:1, 2).

There is no contradiction between the model of a shepherd and the personal model of Jesus. Jesus saw himself as a shepherd in His relationship with people: "I am the good shepherd . . ." (John 10:14). When Jesus functioned as a shepherd, He demonstrated the kind of God we have; for God is man's shepherd, not just his creator (Psalm 23:1). God's people had been so used to being manhandled by their human leaders that they had forgotten the shepherd's heart of God. So Jesus came to make God known to them (John 1:18).

Peter referred to Jesus as being a shepherd and connected that function to His being an overseer (1 Peter 2:25). He also made clear that Jesus was the Chief Shepherd from whom all other overseer-shepherds should take their cues:

> Therefore, I exhort the elders, . . . shepherd the flock of God among you, exercising oversight not under compulsion, but voluntarily, according to the will of God; and not for sordid gain, but with eagerness; nor yet as lording it over those allotted to your charge, but proving to be examples to the flock. And when the Chief Shepherd appears, you will receive the unfading crown of glory (1 Peter 5:1-4).

The model of a shepherd may not say much to us today in this highly industrial age when so many are city dwellers and have never seen a shepherd. How are we to understand what a shepherd does? It would not be appropriate to consider contemporary shepherds, for they are not the ones the inspired writers of the Bible were referring to. Let us look, then, at the model of the shepherd that God intended for us to follow.

ACTIVITIES OF THE SHEPHERDS OF THE BIBLE

1. *The shepherds of the Bible took care of needs.* That is the first thought the Psalmist revealed in talking about God as shepherd: "The Lord is my shepherd, I shall not want" (Psalm 23:1). God knows our needs and takes care of them; the elders of the church need to know the members' needs. This calls for association and communication with them. We can never know another's need unless we know him.

2. *The shepherds rested the flock:* "He makes me lie down in

green pastures" (Psalm 23:2a). Elders need to know when people of the church are overworked. They should not feel that their job is to make "workaholics" out of God's people. God wants us to rest at times. Jesus knew how to get away to rest and how to get His apostles apart for a time of relaxation (Mark 6:31). At times, elders need to say no to people who are overextending themselves. Green pastures describe cool, soft, grassy meadows. They picture for us a refreshing and soothing rest.

3. *The shepherds led the sheep to rest:* "He leads me beside quiet waters" (23:2b). The Hebrew literally says "waters of restfulness." The elders should not only allow their sheep to rest, but also lead them to the place and method of rest. Perhaps an occasional sharing of ideas or helpful suggestions would help the people to know how to rest and relax. Sometimes a relaxing church retreat would help.

For some reason, Americans have come to think it is wrong to be inactive. I have gone to family retreats that have been so filled with activities from sunrise to past a person's normal bedtime that the people go home exhausted. It is a poor shepherd who keeps his flock in a constant run and who can't or won't slow down himself.

4. *The shepherds led the sheep to deep resources.* "Quiet waters" are deep waters; they are not the shallow waters that rush over the rocks and make all the noise. Sheep are afraid of the rapidly running water. Elders need to lead the people into deep studies of God's Word. The surface-only studies leave the people unsatisfied and unhelped spiritually. Every elder should know how to use major Bible tools for studying the Word of God in his own language so he can share and lead his sheep into the depths and help them mature spiritually.

5. *The shepherds restored the sheep.* "He restores my soul" (23:3a). An elder should not keep people down but seek to fulfill a ministry of reconciliation. He is to be an example in living out Galatians 6:1: "Brethren, even if a man is caught in any trespass, you who are spiritual, restore such a one in a spirit of gentleness; looking to yourselves, lest you too be tempted."

The first thought an elder should have when someone

sins—even if that someone is the preacher—is restoration, not revenge or punishment. If the elder's first reaction would be to "fire" him, then he is not being "temperate, gentle, and not pugnacious" (1 Timothy 3:2, 3, qualifications of elders).

6. *The shepherds were leaders of the sheep.* "He guides me in the paths of righteousness for His name's sake" (23:3b). An elder should choose and lead into the right way, not the easy way. And he should do the leading for God's sake, not for himself. People are very much like sheep in that they follow without giving much attention to what they are following, and all have gone astray or turned to their way (Isaiah 53:6). We, as sheep, need leaders in righteousness. We need to be led out of our wrong habits into the fresh and right ways. As sheep, we are often independent and stubborn; so we need strong leadership to see and understand the right way.

7. *The shepherds were companions to the sheep in times of distress.* "Even though I walk through the valley of the shadow of death, I fear no evil; for Thou art with me" (23:4a). The "valley of the shadow of death" is literally the "valley of darkness" and refers to any experiences of deep gloom.

Much like sheep, we occasionally find ourselves in the deep ravines from which the "sunlight" seems to be hiding. We encounter difficulty and danger in life. We don't live on the mountaintops all the time. Beyond every mountain is some kind of valley waiting to be crossed before the next mountain can be scaled. Every person in God's flock experiences such valleys as times of sickness, loneliness, financial loss, loss of job, or times of alienation. The reassuring presence of church elders who really care is needed. Fear can give way to confidence when loneliness is eliminated by fellowship, not by a sermon or a lecture. The valley of darkness is not as scary when we realize that we are not alone in the dark.

8. *The shepherds supported and protected the sheep.* "Thy rod and thy staff, they comfort me" (23:4b). The shepherds' rods were used for defense. There are many who like to lure God's sheep away from His flock. Elders need to be aware of fad teachings that may taste good to the lambs but will poison their minds. The more immature the lambs, the more easily

they can be fooled. Then they become scattered and become "food for every beast" (Ezekiel 34:5). Jesus saw the people as "sheep without a shepherd" (Matthew 9:36).

The shepherd's rod was also used to count the sheep (Ezekiel 20:37). Counting the sheep was done to insure that one had not gone astray from the flock. Elders have a responsibility to count the people of God's flock because they really count. Elders should know who is missing from the worship assembly and be ready to help when needs are apparent.

The shepherd's rod was also used for discipline, and it became a symbolic term for discipline (2 Samuel 7:14; Isaiah 10:5; 11:4; Ezekiel 20:37; Micah 5:1; Psalm 2:9; Proverbs 22:15). Elders should be concerned about disciplining the rebellious sheep—for correction and restoration, not for condemnation and retaliation.

The shepherd's staff was used to help keep the sheep together, and one who had fallen into a pit could be rescued by the shepherd's using the crook on the end. The shepherd would also use the crook to draw a sheep to himself for some special attention.

The elders are to be compassionate and give special attention to God's sheep. If only one wanders off, elders need to gather him back into the fold: "If any man has a hundred sheep, and one of them has gone astray, does he not leave the ninety-nine on the mountains and go and search for the one that is straying?" (Matt. 18:12). Sometimes the total number in attendance at the church meetings takes precedence over the individual ones who are missing. That should never happen in a flock that has concerned shepherds. If my family absents itself from the assembly for a length of time, I should expect that an elder come by in a van to gather us to the assembly on Sunday morning. If I remark, "Mind your own business"; he should reply, "I am. You are my business because I love you."

But if a family in the church moves away, what should we do? We must remember that they are still God's sheep. I am convinced that the elders in a congregation should become active in leading those who move away into getting involved with another flock in their new place of residence. There have been far too many families who have dropped out when they moved because no one actively cared whether they found a new church home or not. Wouldn't it be something if a church had within its budget provisions to send a shepherding elder to the new location to help the family get involved in a new church?

9. *The shepherds provided security for the sheep.* "Thou dost prepare a table before me in the presence of my enemies" (23:5a). There is much in this world that stands opposed to Christianity, and sometimes the opposers are violent. These "enemies" can be close friends, family members, employers, fellow workers, or teachers. In such an environment, few things are more important than for us to know that we are in God's care while in eyesight of our enemies. Any plot of our adversaries will eventually fail. But we will not know the victory is ours if our shepherds ignore us. The elders need to lead the church to surround the lambs with love and fellowship so that a spiritual banquet will continue to be eaten by the sheep, despite their being in enemy territory.

10. *The shepherds soothed the troubled and hurting sheep.* "Thou hast anointed my head with oil; my cup overflows" (Psalm 23:5b). Oil was used to refresh the tired (2 Chronicles 28:15), in daily grooming to give a positive perspective (that is the reason mourners and fasters often neglected using oil— Ruth 3:3; 2 Samuel 12:20; 14:2; Matthew 6:16, 17), and to heal wounds (Luke 10:34). Every Christian will go through troubled and painful circumstances. Sometimes the wounds may even be inflicted by fellow Christians, for we (as sheep) like to butt our heads against each other. Elders need to be aware of the bad times and act as shepherds who bring healing.

11. *The shepherds love their sheep and want good for them.* "Surely goodness and lovingkindness will follow me all the days of my life" (23:6a). The Hebrew for goodness stresses provision for needs. When elders imitate God's character, they will meet the needs of the church people with lovingkindness.

12. *The shepherds want to save their sheep.* "And I will dwell in the house of the Lord forever" (23:6b). Elders will minister to the present needs of the sheep of God's flock with eternity in mind. No good shepherd would want to lose even

one sheep from Heaven. A shepherd would snatch a sheep from the lion's mouth (Amos 3:12), which would call for the elders to go to the source of the temptations and threats that might harm the sheep eternally.

PERVERTED SHEPHERDS

When elders major in minors (such as buildings, finances, and programs) and minor in majors (such as the needs of the people), they become as perverted shepherds—and the sheep become shepherdless. God had much to say about such shepherds, but His basic message was, "Behold I am against the shepherds . . ." (Ezekiel 34:10). Let us discover why.

1. *The shepherds were feeding themselves instead of the flock* (Ezekiel 34:3, 4). They were going to the conventions, clinics, and seminars, but they were not sharing what they had learned. Was it possible that they were afraid the sheep would eventually know as much as they?

"My flock wandered through all the mountains and on every high hill . . ." (34:6). The sheep went from hillside to hillside looking for food, just as some people go from church to church—but in the process they are destroyed (34:5b). The shepherds were irresponsible. They were stupid and did not seek the Lord (Jeremiah 10:20, 21); they had no understanding; they turned to their own way (Isaiah 56:11); they slept through the issues of their day (Nahum 3:8). Thus, they were worthless shepherds (Zechariah 11:17).

2. *The shepherds were not caring for the sheep:* "Those who are sickly you have not strengthened, the diseased you have not healed, the broken you have not bound up, the scattered you have not brought back, nor have you sought for the lost" (Ezekiel 34:4). They were not practically and personally involved in peoples' lives. Strengthening, healing, binding up, bringing back, and seeking cannot happen if elders are elected to function primarily as an official board that meets once a month to make all the decisions. Is it possible that we have elders so overburdened with non-personal concerns that they have no time or energy left over for people's needs? If that happens, we need to rearrange the system. Elders must have

the time to get to know and care for people and have the hearts that will compel them to do so.

3. *The shepherds cared mainly about the power they had over the sheep:* "But with force and with severity you have dominated them" (34:4b). They misunderstood and misused power. Power is not controlling another. Real power comes through serving another. An elder who does not care for people, but loves power, diminishes his influence. The elder who dominates is arrogant and seeks to maintain a privileged position of selfishness. He uses people to increase his own status. God hates people who have such pride (Proverbs 6:16-19), for they destroy and suffocate people instead of developing them. Elders who love things and dominate over people reverse God's creative plan, for God created humans to dominate over things and love people. The devil tempted Adam and Eve to turn that principle around, and he is still at his deceptive game today—even in our churches.

4. *The shepherds did not keep the sheep together:* "And they were scattered for lack of a shepherd, and they became food for every beast of the field and were scattered" (34:5). It is easy to blame the preacher, the times, or the desires of people, when people wander off. We can blame whomever or whatever we want. We can fire the preacher. We can shake our heads at the materialism of our time. But God blamed the shepherds.

We must not claim that our modern lifestyles eliminate the need for shepherds. If God's church is the body of Christ, it needs the head—Christ—and it always will. If God's church is the bride of Christ, it needs the husband, Jesus—and it always will. If God's church is a branch, it needs the vine, Jesus—and it always will. If God's church is His temple, it needs the foundation, Jesus—and it always will. If God's church is His flock, it needs the Chief Shepherd, Jesus—and it always will. And as the church meets in different flocks, it needs human shepherds—and it always will.

THE GOOD SHEPHERDS
Over against the worthless shepherds are the *good*

shepherds. What attributes do good shepherds have that distinguish them from the worthless? Jesus spoke of a few of them.

1. *A good shepherd will be a Christian:* "Truly, truly, I say to you, he who does not enter by the door into the fold of the sheep, but climbs up some other way, he is a thief and a robber. But he who enters by the door is a shepherd of the sheep" (John 10:1, 2).

A person does not become an elder-shepherd because of his influence in the community, but because of his identity with the Christ. Jesus is the door (John 10:9). No man can come to the Father except through Him (14:6), and no one can shepherd His sheep properly unless that one is in Christ.

2. *A good shepherd will know his sheep:* "And the sheep hear his voice, and he calls his own sheep by name" (John 10:3). A shepherd has his own sheep for whom he is responsible (10:14). Too often, we have elders in the church who do not have any sheep assigned to them; thus, their job is narrowed down to a business meeting, presiding at a worship service, or presiding at the Lord's Supper.

To know his sheep, the shepherd must associate with his sheep through such activities as visiting in their homes, telephone calls, and sharing social activities.

3. *A good shepherd leads the sheep:* "And [he] leads them out. When he puts forth all his own, he goes before them, and the sheep follow him because they know his voice" (John 10:3b, 4). A shepherd should lead the sheep, not drive them. He is a shepherd, not a cowboy. They know his voice because he has spent time talking with them.

4. *A good shepherd is trusted by the sheep:* "And a stranger they simply will not follow, but will flee from him, because they do not know the voice of strangers" (John 10:5). We are told that several sheep can be put into the same sleeping space at night and the shepherd will not lose any of his own flock. The sheep from several different flocks may be mingled together, but in the morning, when each shepherd calls his own, the sheep go to their own shepherds. Each sheep will wait until it hears the voice of its own shepherd.

God's shepherds in the church need to teach in such a way that the sheep (members) will trust them so much they will not run after strange voices (religious fads). But before this can happen, the shepherds must be truly concerned about their sheep.

5. *The good shepherd sacrifices for the sheep:* "The good shepherd lays down His life for the sheep" (John 10:11). The good shepherd exists for the good of the sheep; they do not exist for him. Shepherds would literally lie across an open doorway so that any wild beast that tried to get the sheep would have to deal with the shepherd first. A good shepherd will be willing to be hurt for the sake of his sheep. Having that kind of willingness requires real love. However, a counterfeit shepherd (who is a shepherd for status only) will quit when the situation becomes threatening to his own self-image and prestige:

> He who is a hireling, and not a shepherd, who is not the owner of the sheep, beholds the wolf coming, and leaves the sheep, and flees, and the wolf snatches them, and scatters them. He flees because he is a hireling, and is not concerned about the sheep (John 10:12, 13).

Elders must be willing to meet face to face with wolves in lamb's clothing who are making God's sheep their prey. It is the elder's responsibility to confront the cult members who are active in the area—such as the Moonies, the Mormons, and the Jehovah's Witnesses. I wonder how many of the Jim Jones' cult would still be alive if the church had taken the shepherd-sheep concept seriously.

6. *The good shepherd enlarges his flock:* "And I have other sheep, which are not of this fold; I must bring them also" (John 10:16). It would be easy for a shepherd to develop a close relationship with a small group of sheep who love each other so much that they do not want any others to "intrude." But God's shepherds are to realize that God loves the *whole* world and desires that *no one* should perish (John 3:16, 17; 2 Peter 3:9). Thus, they will do all they can to bring others into the flock of God.

SUMMARY

The primary emphasis of the personal and professional model for an overseer or elder in the church is that of a person who cares for others. Paul spotlighted that emphasis when writing about elders. He said, "But if a man does not know how to manage his own household, how will he take care of the church of God?" (1 Timothy 3:5). The words "take care of" come from a Greek word *(epimeleomai)* that stresses looking after people in order to care for their needs. Jesus used the same word to describe the way the good Samaritan looked after the one who had been beaten and robbed (Luke 10:34, 35). It is the good-Samaritan kind of care that the elders are to have for the members of the church.

The model of the shepherd is clearly one who looks after another. He is to help develop healthy sheep for the Chief Shepherd, Jesus. Now we will turn to a consideration of the specifics of how that can be done.

CHAPTER NINE

SPECIFIC FUNCTIONS OF THE ELDERS

While the term "elder" appears in Acts 11:30 to refer to some leaders in the church, it is not the first time that term appears in the book of Acts. Elders were common in Judaism (Acts 4:5, 8, 23; 6:12). They were not a new idea that began with Christianity. Every culture of people has had its council of elders: for example, the Egyptians (Genesis 50:7), the Midians, and the Moabites (Numbers 22:4, 7). Even ancient cities had their elders (Judges 8:14; 11:5; Deuteronomy 19:12). The Greeks had the *gerousia* and *presbsia,* who were the council of older men, the Romans had the Senate, and the Hebrews had their council. Thus, the people in the first century were accustomed to living with a system of elders who gave guidance to and cared for the people.

When Paul and Barnabas finished the evangelistic phase of their first missionary tour (Acts 13:4—14:20), they returned to those cities where they had evangelized (Acts 14:21) and appointed *elders* in every church (Acts 14:23). Paul's first evangelistic efforts in those cities began in the Jewish synagogues (13:14; 14:1). Every synagogue had elders with established qualifications and responsibilities. It is probable that some of his converts were elders in the synagogues; consequently, they would have had an idea of the kind of specific responsibilities necessary to help care for God's new community—the church. For our information and understanding, let us study the functions of the elders in the Scriptures.

FUNCTIONS OF ELDERS IN THE OLD TESTAMENT

1. *Moses acted in the sight of the elders (Exodus 17:6, 7).* No Christian leader is to be independent and do his own thing in

disregard to the people. He is to act in an atmosphere of mutual trust and concern as was between Moses and his council of elders.

2. *Moses taught the elders (Exodus 19:7)*. Becoming an elder does not mean that growth in knowledge and understanding stops. The idea that "I'm an elder now and need not learn from the preacher or anyone else" is not biblical. An elder with that attitude is filled with arrogance, the oppostie of humility (1 Peter 5:1-6).

3. *The elders taught the people (Deuteronomy 32:7)*. This does not mean they were the only ones who taught the people (Exodus 24:1-4), but it does mean that they took the responsibility of teaching seriously. Elders need to be apt to teach.

4. *The elders led in assuring forgiveness of people's sins (Leviticus 4:15; 9:1, 2)*. They prayed for the forgiveness of the people's sins (Deuteronomy 21:6-8). Thus, elders need to be gentle, yet just.

Christians will sin. We need to know that God's forgiveness is as available after we become Christians as before. We need to know that Jesus is our advocate in Heaven (1 John 2:1, 2). Elders should demonstrate an attitude of forgiveness and restoration as well as discipline.

5. *The elders handled disputes among the people—even domestic disputes (Numbers 11:14-17; Deuteronomy 21:18-21; 22:5-21)*. This would have involved counseling. Thus, elders need to be prudent.

Paul criticized Christians in Corinth for taking their disputes against one another to pagan law courts: "I say this to your shame. Is it so, that there is not among you one wise man who will be able to decide between his brethren . . . ?" (1 Cor. 6:5). Shouldn't the church restore the practicalities of being a family and bring membership conflicts to the elders? After all, in many respects, the elders are to function as fathers do. The elders in Judaism were the heads of families, and the elders in the church are to be the heads of families who know how to handle family matters (1 Timothy 3:2, 4). In the Old Testament, elders were sometimes referred to as fathers. To ask for help from the elder was to ask for help from your spiritual father.

6. *The elders disciplined the rebellious (Deuteronomy 19:11-13; 21:18-21).* Both Jesus and Paul made it clear that discipline is also to be a part of the New Testament church (Matthew 18:15-20; Romans 16:16, 17; 1 Corinthians 5:1-8; 2 Thessalonians 3:6-15; 1 Timothy 1:18-20; Titus 3:10, 11; Jude). This aspect will be examined more closely in the next chapter, "Discipline in the Church."

7. *The elders evaluated what was causing weaknesses and tried to reverse it (1 Samuel 4:3).* Elders need to help build up the body of Christ (Ephesians 4:11-16). To do that, they need to evaluate hindrances and be example-setters.

8. *The elders selected leaders (Judges 11:5-11; 2 Samuel 3:17).* Elders need to look for potential among people and enlist capable people to be leaders. There are many areas of service that people need to be challenged with and recruited to.

9. *The elders helped grieving persons (2 Samuel 12:17).* God continues to comfort us in order that we might comfort others (2 Corinthians 1:3-6). Elders should be willing to extend comfort and compassion to those who are grieving.

10. *The elders reminded the people of God's Word when the people began to make decisions without regard to it (Jeremiah 26:17, 18).* This need never ceases. Elders must be committed to the Word and be able to exhort their flocks as well as be able to refute those who contradict God's Word (Titus 1:9).

11. *The elders asked the congregation for advice (Judges 21:16).* Elders are not to function in isolation from the assembly. In order to function *for* the family of God and yet be *with* them, the elders must not act as lords *over* the people (Titus 1:7; 1 Peter 5:3).

12. *The elders delegated responsibilities to others (1 Samuel 11:3).* Every member of the body of Christ is to be a functioning part (1 Corinthians 12:12-31). No one group or individual can do all the work. Part of the elders' responsibility is to use others in the work of the ministry (Ephesians 4:12). It is only as every member is functioning that the body is properly built up (Ephesians 4:16). Thus, the elders should not be threatened when others function in some areas better than they do. There

is no room for elders who think they must be superior to everyone else.

13. *The elders made mistakes (1 Samuel 8:4, 5).* The elders of the Hebrews asked for a king so they could be like all the other nations around them. This action was a mistake.

Because elders are human and fallible, they should function *with* the congregation, not just over them. They should understand the people and realize that disagreement with the decision of the elders may not be a sign of rebellion. It may be that the elders have made a mistake and may need to re-evaluate their decision.

The people of God served well as long as faithful elders functioned well: "And the people served the Lord all the days of Joshua, and all the days of the elders who survived Joshua, who had seen all the great work of the Lord which He had done for Israel" (Judges 2:7). Evidently, the surviving elders continued to care for the people in a variety of ways, which included teaching truths.

However, something happened when those elders died: "And all that generation also were gathered to their fathers; and there arose another generation after them who did not know the Lord, nor yet the work which He had done for Israel. Then the sons of Israel did evil in the sight of the Lord, and served the Baals, and they forsook the Lord . . ." (Judges 2:10-12).

What happened? Evidently, the next generation of elders did not take their leadership responsibilities seriously. It is so easy to look back on the "good, ole' days" and think everything will be okay because it once was. One group of good elders who function properly does not guarantee that the succeeding group will do the same. Each elder is responsible to function properly; it is a work that he is called to do.

Christianity is like a relay race. We pass the baton on from one generation to the next. The race is often won or lost in the passing of the baton. A church that selects elders who do not desire the work or who are not qualified makes a serious mistake, for the church cannot rise above her leaders. It is a grievous mistake for anyone in the church to take the eldership lightly. Jeremiah grieved when the people did not favor elders (Lamentations 4:16; 5:12) and when the elders remained silent when they should have spoken (Lamentations 2:9, 10).

FUNCTIONS OF JEWISH ELDERS IN THE NEW TESTAMENT

Jewish elders in the New Testament seemed more concerned about the institution and about self security than about the needs of the people. They maintained order in the synagogue service. From Jewish sources, we learn that elders in the synagogue delegated someone to preside and regulated the finances by receiving and dispersing the monies. It may have been an elder that invited Paul and Barnabas to speak in the synagogue (Acts 13:15).

But for the most part, the elders opposed Jesus and Christianity. They questioned the authority of Jesus (Matthew 21:23), planned His killing (Matthew 26:3, 4; 27:1), sent people to arrest Him (26:47), paid Judas to betray Him (27:3), persuaded the crowd to ask for Barabbas (27:20), mocked Jesus when He was on the cross (27:40, 41), helped pay the soldiers to lie about the resurrection (28:12, 13), tried to stop the apostolic preaching (Acts 4:5, 8, 18), supported a terrorist hunger strike because of their determination to kill Paul (Acts 23:14), and brought charges against Paul (Acts 24:1).

Elders today can also stand in God's way if they act as the heads of the body of Christ instead of allowing the risen Lord to be the head.

FUNCTIONS OF CHRISTIAN ELDERS IN THE NEW TESTAMENT

We do not have a multitude of references that show us what the Christian elders did specifically. That is why it is important for us to glean an understanding from the example of Jesus, the functions and attitudes of shepherds, and the faithfulness of the Jewish elders in the Old Testament. However, the few New Testament references are very helpful.

1. *The Christian elders helped the hungry.* When Barnabas and Saul brought relief to those affected by the famine in Jerusalem, they brought the money to the elders (Acts 11:30). Why? Because as shepherds, elders would be concerned about

any need the people had. The idea that elders are to care for the spiritual needs while the deacons take care of the physical needs is simply not Biblical.

Where did the elders in the Jerusalem church come from? It is possible that they were selected in Acts 6:1-6. While many see these seven men who were selected in this passage as the first deacons, the text does not call them deacons. In fact, the text does not give them any title—only a function. Some early Christian writers saw them as elders (Eusebius, Chrysostom). We do know that men were selected in Acts 6, and in Acts 11 there were elders in that church who were performing a similar function—caring for the people's needs. Yet we have no mention of deacons being in the Jerusalem church in any portion of the book of Acts.

2. *The Christian elders discussed doctrinal issues (Acts 15).* The elders discussed an issue by considering various men's experiences and by studying Scripture (15:6-21). They made their decision *with* the church (v. 22).

Many of the doctrinal issues that divide us today might have been settled years ago had we had the commitment and courage to spend the necessary time in study and discussion to work through the issues.

3. *The Christian elders continued to be built up by the Word of God and His grace (Acts 20:32).* Elders must be in the daily process of becoming more and more like Jesus. Their growth in the spiritual realm must never stop.

4. *The Christian elders had to be on guard for themselves (Acts 20:28).* Elders can make mistakes and can be carried away from the Lord as surely as anyone else. They must constantly guard against it.

5. *The Christian elders were to shepherd the church of God (Acts 20:28).* This meant extending care, comfort, compassion, and protection for the members.

6. *The Christian elders were to watch out for perverted elders (Acts 20:29, 31).* Because sheep follow their shepherds, the elders must be willing to purge their own number of perverted leadership.

7. *The Christian elders maintained the unity and peace with-*

out compromising the essentials of their faith (Acts 21:18-26). The elders advised Paul to participate in a Jewish activity for the purpose of correcting misunderstandings and maintaining unity between the Jewish and Gentile Christians. These elders were flexible and not concreted to one method of doing things when that method was not tied to salvation. Elders today need that same kind of flexibility.

8. *The Christian elders cared for the household of God (1 Timothy 3:5; 5:17).* Some may feel that the words "manage" and "rule" used in these verses in 1 Timothy mean "control." These words come from the same Greek word *(proistemi)* which means to manage by giving help or care.

Paul made that connection when he wrote "take care of" as a parallel to "manage": "But if a man does not know how to manage his own household, how will he take care of the church of God" (1 Timothy 3:5). We have already seen the Greek word for "take care of" is the same as used to describe the action of the good Samaritan (Luke 10:34, 35).

9. *The Christian elders worked hard at preaching and teaching (1 Timothy 5:17).* The Greek word for "worked hard" *(kopiao)* stressed getting tired. Many elders literally wore themselves out "in the Word" and teaching.

Unless elders continue to do that, the church can be taken on a wild ride in theology by an evangelist (a local one, one traveling through, or one on the electronic media). With the constant rise of all sorts of cults, elders may have to be working harder than ever "in the Word."

10. *The Christian elders ministered to the sick* (James 5:14, 15). Paul was probably referring to this kind of ministry when he reminded the elders at Ephesus that they must "help the weak" (Acts 20:35). The word *weak* here is the same Greek word that is translated "sick" in James 5:14.

Christianity has been divided over the specific details of this text while missing the major thrust, which is that elders are to demonstrate personal care for the sick as a shepherd would for sick lambs. Oil was commonly used for medical purposes and later began to be connected with magical healings by pagans. James corrected that idea. He assumed that caring for the sick would involve use of oil, but commanded the elders to *pray* for the sick. He connected whatever benefits resulted to the prayers that were said. Literally James wrote, "they must pray upon them after (or while) anointing with oil . . ." Anointing with oil is not a command, but it was being done.

The word for anointing *(aleipho)* is not the same word that is reserved to refer to religious anointing *(chrio)*. Any time this second word is used, it refers only to a religious act (Luke 4:18; Acts 4:27; 10:38; 2 Corinthians 1:21; Hebrews 1:9). The word James used refers to rubbing ointment on a person as a medicine without regard to any religious or sacred act (Mark 16:1).

What does this tell us about the elders' responsibilities? There are two possible understandings. One is that the oil James refers to is used for medical purposes, thus the elders were functioning somewhat as medical missionaries do today by combining medicine with prayer. Elders who are concerned about the sick should not neglect the medicine the doctor has prescribed nor the prayer which God prescribes. God and doctors do not have to be competitors; they should be partners. And the elders should be partners with the doctors as well.

The second understanding is that regardless of the culture, oil should be used along with the prayers. Elders would not be wrong to use the oil in this way. However, we must be cautious in thinking that healing will always follow (James 5:15). If that were James' point, physical death could be eliminated by following this formula. Paul could have gotten rid of his ailment (but he did not, 2 Corinthians 12:8, 9) and would not have had to leave a man sick on his journey (2 Timothy 4:20).

James' point is that the prayers, not the oil, are effective in the healing. To do this "in the name of the Lord" is to do it as God's representative who is willing to leave the result in the hands of God.

11. *The Christian elders were examples to the congregation (1 Peter 5:3).* Since the members of the congregation are as sheep who follow leaders, the elders need to be the kind of examples that will lead the members to Jesus in attitudes and actions. Elders need to be more concerned about being ex-

amples than about being executives. Executives can work apart from their subordinates, but example-setters can be effective only as they live with and among the people. This calls for involvement.

A SUMMARY

It takes spiritual maturity to look upon people's needs, and such care provides the finest basis for influencing people. Elders are to be the leaders in seeing that whatever needs a member of God's family has are met. Such caring will include the following:

1. Resting the flock
2. Providing deep resources
3. Restoring souls
4. Leading in righteousness
5. Being a companion in distress
6. Being a protector and supporter
7. Disciplining
8. Comforting
9. Providing security
10. Soothing the troubled and hurting
11. Being able to be taught
12. Being able to teach others
13. Forgiving
14. Handling disputes
15. Evaluating weaknesses
16. Selecting leaders
17. Helping the grieving
18. Reminding the people of God's Word
19. Asking the congregation for advice
20. Delegating responsibilities
21. Knowing they can make mistakes too
22. Discussing doctrinal issues
23. Continuing to grow
24. Guarding self
25. Shepherding the church
26. Purging perverted elders
27. Being flexible
28. Preserving unity without compromising the essentials
29. Preaching and teaching
30. Ministering to the sick
31. Being examples
32. Knowing the people
33. Leading the people
34. Being trustworthy
35. Making sacrifices for the people
36. Enlarging the flock

CHAPTER TEN

DISCIPLINE IN THE CHURCH

Discipline is as important in the family of God as it is in the families of men. In fact, in a sense, all of the New Testament epistles are disciplinary letters. The Greek word for "discipline" *(paideia)* stresses bringing someone up from immaturity to maturity.

There are two categories of discipline: preventive and corrective. Preventive discipline is teaching a person the correct way in order to keep the person from erring. It is done by teaching with words, by association, and by modeling. Each of us was trained in this way. We learned from watching the lives of our parents and older brothers and/or sisters and from our parents' direct teaching with words. In Christianity, this type of discipline is accomplished by fellowship, by teaching, and by preaching. Jesus used this type of discipline with His disciples. They went with Him on His trips, observed His attitudes, and listened to His words. We are all familiar with this type of discipline, but we often fail to think of it as "discipline."

Corrective discipline is steering a person into the correct way when he is erring. It is done by teaching, rebuking, modeling, and by punishment. We are all familiar with this type of discipline, but there is one expression of this discipline that is Biblical, yet often neglected and/or misunderstood when used in the church. Withdrawing fellowship from a member is the expression of corrective discipline that we shall consider in the remainder of this chapter.

The following texts should be studied carefully, for they are the foundation for an understanding of this expression of corrective discipline as used in the church: Matthew 18:15-20; Romans 16:16, 17; 1 Corinthians 5:1-13; 2 Corinthians 2:5-11; 2

Thessalonians 3:6-15; 1 Timothy 1:18-20; Titus 3:10, 11; Revelation 2:20.

Clarifying the Issue. Discipline is not a term used just for kicking someone out of the church after an unrepented error. It is a term that also includes helping a person get out of temptation and error. Although discipline may be viewed as negative, it should be expressed in a positive way. It is positive to help a person see a dangerous situation and offer alternatives for help. Alexander Campbell wrote that discipline of the church of Jesus Christ is as necessary and of as much importance to its peace, purity, and unity as the administration of any government on earth *(Millennial Harbinger,* III, p. 562). He also wrote,

> To cut off an offender is good, to cure him is better, but to prevent him falling is best of all. The Christian Spirit and system alike inculgate vigilence in preventing, all expedition in healing offenses, and all firmness in removing incorrigible *(The Christian System,* p. 69).

Who should be removed from the fellowship? A member who is in a continual sexual sin from which he will not repent (1 Corinthians 5:1-5), a member who continues to be factious and will not change (Titus 3:10, 11; Romans 16:17; Jude 15-19), a member who openly confesses that he will continue to disobey apostolic truth when he knows it to be apostolic truth (2 Thessalonians 3:14, 15), and a member who refuses to work for support when he is able to work and work is available (2 Thessalonians 3:6-15) are the only clear-cut cases we have in Scripture. I concur with Alexander Campbell, who wrote:

> No person ought ever to be excluded from the church of Jesus Christ for anything said or done by him unless the gospel shows that his conduct would exclude him from heaven *(Millennial Harbinger,* III, p. 563).

Extreme caution must be exercised when utilizing corrective discipline in the church. Campbell also observed, "Whenever a church proceeds to censure, condemn, or exclude for difference of opinion or through passion, prejudice, or ignorance, discipline is rendered useless" *(Millennial Harbinger,* III, p. 562). Too often, men in places of authority want to render discipline by removal just because people do not agree with them. To do that sets up human popes in the congregation.

Paul did not immediately think about disfellowshipping people because they did not agree with him. He did not even think about removal immediately when people were sinning. Instead he wrote letters, prayed, made personal visits, and sent his helpers to be with the erring people. Discipline by removal was the *last* thing he wanted to do. Prior to any decision to remove someone from the church must come vigorous activity for reconciliation (Matthew 18:15-20). To bypass the reconciliation is to be more interested in the condemnation of someone than the salvation of that person.

The Purpose of Removal. We should do it as brothers, not as enemies (2 Thessalonians 3:15). We should do it to save the person, not to destroy him (1 Corinthians 5:5). To "destroy the flesh" means the sinful works of the flesh. We should do it to lead a person to repentance. Restoration can follow true repentance (2 Corinthians 2:6-8). We should also do it to prevent the leavening effect of the person's actions, which can capture the whole body (1 Corinthians 5:6, 7). Seth Wilson said it well, "To discipline a person is not to put him out of the reach of God's mercy, but rather it is to usher him out of the range of assurance and comfort (Ozark Bible College *Compass,* October, 1975).

The Process of Removal (Matthew 18:15-17). Go to the erring brother or sister in private. If he or she repents, that is enough. No one else need know about the situation. If he will not repent, take two or three witnesses. If he then repents, that is enough. If he will not repent, even when he has been given time to realize the need of discipline, he should then be treated as an outsider, which means disfellowship. Who should make this decision? It is probably wise for the elders to make it and for it to be carried out by the congregation.

The Power of This Discipline. People need people; thus, this discipline wields tremendous power. We use this discipline when we do not allow our children to participate with their friends in activities as a means of punishment. Many parents today call it "grounding." Or it is somewhat the same as sending a child to his room for the rest of the evening, preventing him from participating in the family's activities.

I can remember being disciplined in this way. I threatened to run away in order to get my own way (ever have anyone in the church threaten to leave unless he got his way?); I just knew it would work. My folks did not say a word; so I got on my bike and rode away; I didn't even bother to get a clean shirt. After I rode for a couple of hours, the hunger pangs began and I could visualize what the rest of the family would be having for supper and for breakfast the next morning. I soon realized that I needed my family more than I needed getting my own way. When I got home, there was a plate waiting on the table for me.

SUMMARY

The discipline in the church can work much the same way on the erring person. When the church "winks at" sin, the maturing process of the members can be hindered. We need to take sin seriously and help people with love to grow into spiritual maturity. At the same time, we must not pollute the purpose of this form of discipline by removing persons and then feeling proud that the church is "pure."

A preacher friend of mine confessed to me that he spanked his one-week-old daughter; he thought that was the way to straighten out a new infant. How wrong he was! And how wrong we are when we fail to distinguish rebellion and unrepentant attitudes from spiritual immaturity. There is a difference between wickedness and weakness. People are at different levels of spiritual growth. The church must be willing to put up with crybabies and to change some dirty diapers. To bypass that by throwing the babies out when the first stink arises will bypass growth in spirituality.

CHAPTER ELEVEN

QUALIFICATIONS AND SELECTION OF THE ELDERS

How can any person possibly fulfill all the elder's functions that we discussed in the last few chapters? What kind of person are we talking about, anyway? Let us now consider what qualifications such a person needs.

THE PURPOSE

The qualifications cannot be divorced from the functions of the elders and should not be studied until the functions are clearly in mind. The Holy Spirit, through Paul, did not derive a set of qualifications merely at random or with no thought to their practical value. Qualifications for any job are related to the responsibilities of that job. It would be irrelevant to reject a person for a certain job because he did not fulfill some arbitrary qualification that had nothing to do with the performance of his job. For instance, to refuse to hire a mathematics teacher because he cannot run a mile in five minutes would be ridiculous. However, refusing to hire a basketball player for that reason would make sense.

It is also extremely unkind to put a person in a job for which he is not qualified. If his aptitudes don't apply to that job, he will fail. He will be depressed and have low self-esteem. His future usefulness will be impaired. Before I was sent to air traffic controller school in the Air Force, I was given an aptitude test. I was sent to that school because the Air Force knew the functions of an air traffic controller and knew that my aptitudes fit those functions.

Our Lord knows the functions of an elder and the aptitudes

necessary to fulfill them, and He has shared that knowledge with us. A man who does not have those aptitudes will not be able to fulfill the functions of an elder. This does not mean that he is not a good Christian man. It does not mean he is second-rate. But just because a man is a good Christian does not mean he is suited to do any job available in the church.

One of the problems that has plagued the church is that we have often reduced the work of an elder to sitting at the Lord's table, to praying in public, and to meeting once a month in a board meeting. People see the position as one of status, and election to the office is a kind of reward. When we reduce the eldership to that, it is little wonder that any man thinks he can do the job and feels slighted if he is not selected. Certainly the Scriptural qualifications are not necessary for a man to pass out communion trays and to make business decisions.

What we must do is talk to the men about the functions of an elder first; then show how the qualifications fit the job. If a man does not qualify, he is available to do another type of ministry in the church for which he is better suited. Putting the wrong man into the eldership will result in failure, embarrass-ment, and disappointment in himself. Thus, the qualifications in the Scripture are protecting the man as much as the church.

It is commendable that men want to be elders. But desire alone is not sufficient reason for selecting a man. Paul em-phasized that when he said, "If any man aspires to the office of overseer, it is a fine work he desires to do" (1 Timothy 3:1). The word for "aspire" means to reach out after something for the purpose of drawing it to oneself. Some men could be reaching out for the eldership for the wrong reasons and with the wrong qualifications. Perhaps a man wants to be an elder so he can have status. Perhaps he would like to control and have power over others, instead of to serve and lead them. Paul even said that some elders in Ephesus would become like wolves, not sparing the flock, speaking perverse things, and drawing peo-ple after them (Acts 20:29, 30).

Such things had probably begun to happen by the time Paul wrote to Timothy; so he reminded them that anyone who as-pires to eldership (the word office is not in the Greek) is desiring a good work. The word *good* stresses both quality and usefulness. The word *work* stresses deeds. The eldership is work and it takes certain aptitudes to fulfill it. Thus, Paul said immediately, "An overseer, then, must be . . ." and listed the qualifications. Notice the word *must*. These qualifications are not optional or just nice attitudes to aim toward—they are necessary to do the work.

THE QUALIFICATIONS

We turn to the Scriptures now to discover the qualities that God desires to be within the life and character of elders.

> A. 1 Timothy 3:2-7: "An overseer, then, must be above reproach, the husband of one wife, temperate, prudent, respectable, hospitable, able to teach, not addicted to wine or pugnacious, but gentle, uncontentious, free from the love of money. He must be one who manages his own household well, keeping his children under control with all dignity (but if a man does not know how to manage his own household, how will he take care of the church of God?); and not a new convert, lest he become conceited and fall into the condemnation incurred by the devil. And he must have a good reputation with those outside the church, so that he may not fall into reproach and the snare of the devil.

1. *"Above reproach."* This does not mean that a man is never criticized nor reproached. Jesus was "reproached" many times. The word *reproach* literally means *taken hold of*. It stresses the fact that charges against a man will not *stick* when all the evidence is in.

2. *"The husband of one wife."* Literally, the Greek says, "a one-woman man." Christians will continue to argue about whether or not a man who has ever been divorced can be an elder. In my judgment, this phrase is not just describing a man's marital situation, but his whole attitude. It is possible for a man to be married to the same woman for fifty years and still not be a one-woman man. Being such a man demands a faithfulness, a total responsibility. A man may not cheat on his wife but still not have the commitment he should have. He may not meet her needs or love her as Christ loves the church.

If we require that this qualification has to be present throughout the man's total adult life, we must make that true for all the other qualifications as well. To do that does not account for growth from a babe in Christ to maturity or God's forgiveness or a man's repentance. Instead, I think we must consider all the qualifications from the standpoint of a man's present life-style. We must allow room for God to change people and not lock a person into his life-style of ten years ago.

This text calls for marriage as a necessity. There are practical reasons for that. A man who has not had experience in leading a human family would be too inexperienced to lead God's family of the church. There are experiences involving interpersonal relationships in a marriage that are indispensible in knowing how to handle relationships in the church. A person who has not been married can never fully understand or adequately counsel families without experiencing marriage himself. I did not believe that when I was single, but I do now.

3. *"Temperate."* A temperate person is a well-balanced person. He is stable and does not go to extremes. He does not shift with the winds; he stands firm in his beliefs.

4. *"Prudent."* A prudent person has a sound mind. He uses discretion and has a purpose behind his actions. His mind is under control.

5. *"Respectable."* This word comes from the Greek term which means *order (kosmos)*. It pictures a man who has his morals in order. He is an honorable person ethically.

6. *"Hospitable."* Literally, he is "a lover of strangers." He will be a person who is open to others, even those outside of his group.

7. *"Able to teach."* He understands truth and is able to communicate it.

8. *"Not addicted to wine."* The Greek is literally, *not beside wine,* which carries the idea that he does not linger long beside the wine. He does not need it to keep going. He is not a drunkard.

9. *"Not pugnacious."* This literally means *not a fighter.* He is not a hothead. He does not love disputes, debates, and strife.

10. *"Gentle."* He is able to put up with circumstances. He is able to yield; he is mild and kind. We should never forget that kindness is desirable in a man (Proverbs 19:22).

11. *"Uncontentious."* The Greek literally says, "Averse to fighting." He is not quarrelsome. He radiates the spirit of peace.

12. *"Free from the love of money."* The Greek literally says, "Not a friend of money." He is a man who believes he is a steward of money and uses it wisely but not selfishly.

13. *"Manages his own household well."* The word *manage* was used to describe one who steered a ship. It also stresses someone who leads by caring for people.

The man's role in the human family is the best training ground and checkpoint for the eldership. How a man steers his family is probably how he will steer God's family members. Perhaps one of the best ways to develop potential elders is to spend time developing better husbands and fathers.

14. *"Not a new convert."* He is not a novice in the faith; he is not a babe in Christ.

15. *"A good reputation with those outside the church."* The Greek literally says, "A good witness from those outside." He is a man who is involved in the secular world without letting it influence him or take him away from God's way.

> B. Titus 1:6-9: ". . . If any man be above reproach, the husband of one wife, having children who believe, not accused of dissipation or rebellion. For the overseer must be above reproach as God's steward, not self-willed, not quick-tempered, not addicted to wine, not pugnacious, not fond of sordid gain, but hospitable, loving what is good, sensible, just, devout, self-controlled, holding fast the faithful word which is in accordance with the teaching, that he may be able both to exhort in sound doctrine and to refute those who contradict."

For this passage of Scripture, we will consider those qualifications that are listed here but were not in the 1 Timothy passage.

1. *"Having children who believe."* A man without children who are old enough to believe has not had enough experience in developing maturing children; consequently, he may not have the experience it takes to help develop spiritually matur-

ing children of God. Only by experience or by direct inspiration (as with Jesus) can a man know how to handle properly two feuding children, whether they are children fighting over a toy or two adults fighting over a piano at the church building.

2. *"Above reproach as God's stewards."* An elder is responsible to God; he is not to do "his own thing."

3. *"Not self-willed."* A self-willed person does what pleases himself. He is so pleased with his own opinions that nothing else pleases him. He is stubborn and will not be persuaded by others. An elder should not be this selfish or stubborn.

4. *"Not quick-tempered."* The Greek word *(orgitos)* describes someone who is quick to blow up, impulsive. This should not describe an elder.

5. *"Not pugnacious."* A different Greek word is used here than what is used in 1 Timothy 3. This word literally means *not a striker.* He will turn the other cheek. He will not slander when slandered. He does not seek revenge.

6. *"Not fond of sordid gain."* This describes a man who does not need material gain to be satisfied.

7. *"Loving what is good."* This involves loving *quality* in every aspect of life.

8. *"Sensible."* This is the same word as "prudent" in the Timothy passage.

9. *"Just."* This person is fair and upright. His judgments can be trusted. He is careful about his duties to his fellowmen.

10. *"Devout."* The Greek word *(osios)* is often coupled with *just.* While the just man is careful about his duties toward his fellowmen, the devout man is careful about his duties toward God.

11. *"Self-controlled."* This person is not controlled by his environment. He does not "go with the flow." He is self-disciplined and has an inner power.

12. *"Holding fast the faithful word."* This person knows the Word of God and is committed to it, can teach it to others, and can refute those who contradict the Word.

CONNECTING THE QUALIFICATIONS AND THE FUNCTIONS

The qualifications outlined in Scripture enable a man to fulfill the elder's functions that are also revealed in Scripture. The following chart will clarify what qualifications help the elder perform certain functions (this is only a partial listing; it might be helpful if you continued the matching):

The Function	The Qualifications Needed
1. Resting the people	temperate, prudent, manage own household, sensible
2. Providing deep resources	apt to teach, not a new convert, holds fast to the Word
3. Leading in right-eousness	above reproach, lover of good, devout, good reputation, respectable
4. Forgiving	not quick tempered, not pugnacious
5. Handling disputes	manage own household well, temperate, prudent, sensible, just
6. Asking congregation for advice	not self-willed, uncontentious, prudent
7. Discussing doctrinal issues	holding fast to the Word, not self-willed, not a new convert
8. Being a companion in distress	hospitable, gentle, manage household
9. Being flexible	self-controlled, not self-willed, uncontentious, manage household
10. Making sacrifices for the peace	not a lover of money, manage own household, uncontentious
11. Ministering to the sick	gentle, lover of good, hospitable, manage household

We cannot approach these qualifications as if we were in a cafeteria serving line—taking what we like and leaving the rest. The kindest and most protective thing we can do for both the man and the church is to expect the elder to have these qualities. Proverbs gives us excellent insight into what happens when a man or a group of people have these qualities or do not have them. Following is a brief listing and consideration of what Proverbs makes clear will happen when a quality is absent or present:

1. *Prudent-sensible.* The opposite of a prudent man is a fool. Proverbs says, "A fool's mouth is his ruin, And his lips are the snare of his soul" (18:7). When a fool is present, both the individual and the group get hurt. "Let a man meet a bear

robbed of her cubs, rather than a fool in his folly" (17:12). Does anyone want to go to a fool for counseling or discipline?

The fool rushes in where angels fear to tread. "Like one who takes a dog by the ears Is he who passes by and meddles with strife not belonging to him" (26:17). It takes a wise elder to know when to let things alone. The unwise elder thinks he has to be in the middle of everything. Anyone want to grab a strange German shepherd dog by the ears? Who will get hurt—the dog or the grabber? We set a man up to get hurt if we put him into a position that requires prudence when he does not have it. (See also 13:14, 16; 14:1; 15:2, 7, 14, 21; 16:23; 17:2, 18, 24; 18:2, 6, 15; 19:11; 22:3; 24:3-6; 26:4, 5; 27:12; 29:8.)

2. *Not pugnacious.* "Through presumption comes nothing but strife" (13:10). Do we want continuous battles being waged in the church? "Sweetness of speech increases persuasiveness" (16:21). An elder must be able to lead by persuasion and sweet, kind speech. If he cannot, he will lose the respect of the people. (See also 1:19; 11:9; 12:18; 14:30; 15:1, 4; 17:14; 18:19; 19:22; 20:3; 26:20; 30:14).

3. *Uncontentious.* "When pride comes, then comes dishonor" (11:2). We do not want a man to come to dishonor. (See also 1:5; 12:15; 15:22; 16:18, 25; 18:12; 19:20; 21:4; 25:14; 26:12; 28:25, 26; 29:23.)

4. *Temperate.* "He who gives an answer before he hears, It is folly and shame to him" (18:13). Notice who gets hurt. Surely we don't want to make a man open to folly and shame. "He who guards his mouth and his tongue, Guards his soul from troubles" (21:23). Until a man can be temperate with his mouth, we are doing him a favor by not making him an elder. (See also 19:2, 14; 20:25; 21:5, 9; 21:19; 25:15.)

5. *Not quick tempered.* "A quick-tempered man acts foolishly" (14:17). He also "exalts folly" (14:29), and people will know it. He will be known as a fool, rather than as a man of honor. People do not respect fools. A quick-tempered elder can cause others' tempers to rise, and soon the whole church is known by its fights and shouting matches. "Do not associate with a man given to anger; Or go with a hot-tempered man,

Lest you learn his ways, And find a snare for yourself" (22:24, 25). (See also 17:14, 27; 19:19; 22:10; 26:20, 21; 29:8.)

6. *Not a lover of money.* People will curse the stingy man, but the generous man will prosper (11:25, 26). That will also happen to a stingy and generous congregation. A congregation's attitude and actions with money are largely conditioned by its leaders. God expects congregations to be generous in sharing resources. The man (or congregation) who puts too much priority on money will fail (11:28). The man (or congregation) that is gracious to the poor will be happy (14:21). Not caring for the poor is a reproach to God (14:31), while giving to the poor is making a loan to God (19:17). Probably much potential good lies undeveloped and unexpressed because of a congregation's attitude about money. Selecting stingy elders is one of the worst things a congregation can do for the man, the church, and the Lord. (See also 11:24; 17:5; 21:13; 22:9; 23:4-7; 28:8, 16, 27; 30:8, 9, 15.)

7. *Manage household.* An elder must be wise in all of his relationships and have all his priorities in the right balance (6:1-5; 11:15; 14:15, 18). How a man has handled his family relationships and his obligations reveals a great deal about his inner character and his wisdom in making decisions. If he cannot have a good relationship with those in his neighborhood, if he has difficulty getting along with those at home, or if he does not handle his financial obligations well, he will make trouble in the church.

8. *Respectable, above reproach.* A man who loves strife and gossip will destroy relationships within the church (16:28; 17:19). A man who is unselfish and is an example of righteousness will be building up the church, not tearing it down.

9. *Hospitable.* A person who separates himself from others is selfish; he is only concerned with his own interests (18:1, 2). He will not be able to reach out to others with care and concern as an elder-shepherd should do. The best way to lose an enemy is to reach out to him in warmth and hospitality (25:21, 22).

10. *Able to teach.* It is a great virtue to have wisdom and understanding (1:2-7), and victory and guidance result when a

person is able to communicate that wisdom and understanding to others (11:14). A person who studies the Word of God and shares it will find good (16:20). A wise man will also listen to counsel as well as be ready to give it (12:15). All of these aspects are essential as elders seek to instruct and guide the congregation.

11. *Not given to wine.* Wine drinking brings fighting, foolishness, poverty, laziness, sorrow, contentions, incapacitation of the mind and body, and loss of self-control. No church needs such problems. (See 20:1; 21:17; 23:20, 21, 29-35; 31:4-7.)

12. *Gentle.* Being kind makes one approved in the sight of both men and God (3:3, 4). A sweet, kind person can persuade others (16:21). Kindness is a very desirable trait in God's view (19:22), and it is certainly essential for elders, who need to be able to handle relationships.

13. *Self-controlled.* A person who can control his temper brings peace, while one who cannot brings strife (15:18). An uncontrolled person is as defenseless as a city without walls (25:28). One who cannot control his tongue will only come to ruin (13:3). A controlled person knows the value in stopping an argument before it goes too far (17:14). To have peace and harmony in a congregation, elders with this quality are invaluable.

14. *Loving what is good.* God is a guard and shield to those who are upright and full of integrity (2:7, 8); a righteous man will bless and be blessed (8:32-34; 20:7); loyalty and truth are a part of goodness and righteousness (20:28). God would rather have us be righteous than to keep our rituals (21:3); honor will come to the good man (21:21). On the other hand, evil men cause trouble and violence (24:1, 2). Righteousness exalts, while sin disgraces (14:34). One who is to lead in righteousness should certainly be an example of righteousness.

15. *Sensible.* Discretion delivers a person (or church) from evil men and evil ways (2:11-22). A person who has insight will be respected, while one who does not will be despised (12:8). A fool is selfish and does not desire understanding (18:2). Elders must certainly seek the respect of the people they lead

and be protected from evil because of their sensibleness and prudence.

16. *Just.* A righteous man will be able to guide others (12:26); wise judgment demands justice and righteousness (18:5). There is joy in justice if one is righteous, but justice is a terror to those in sin (21:15). A just person will rebuke the wicked, not side with or cover up for them; he who sides with the wicked will be cursed and abhorred (24:23-25). "Like one who binds a stone in a sling, so is he who gives honor to a fool" (26:8). An unjust elder will not help the church advance or be able to guide others into righteousness. (See also 28:5, 12, 21; 29:2, 4, 7, 27.)

SELECTION OF ELDERS

Many congregations spend more time and effort selecting the color for the paint in the classrooms of the church building than they spend selecting the elders. Too often, the time for the election of elders slips up on us, and we hurriedly make up a list of qualifications and men, place them on the ballot at the last minute, and have the congregation vote one Sunday morning without advance notice or preparation. This is hardly fitting for such an important job in the life of a congregation!

Here are some suggestions for preparing the congregation and the men for the selection of elders:

1. At least six months prior to selecting the elders, involve the entire congregation in a special study that deals with the nature of the church, the nature of Biblical leadership, and the function and qualifications of elders.

2. Determine a method that would suit your congregation of how to find potential elders. The method would depend upon the size and make-up of the congregation, how scattered the membership is, and how closely the church members fellowship. It is imperative that the men who are known to have the qualifications and desire the job be selected. People who do not really know the men can hardly vote intelligently for the elders. It would also be important that the people know the Biblical functions of elders in order to choose wisely. It would be helpful to allow the whole congregation to suggest names

of those who they feel could do the job properly instead of restricting the nomination list to a nominating committee's suggestions.

It is important that everyone who suggests a name knows the man *and* his family life. The character of the members of his family should be considered as well as his conduct and attitude in his home. He may be quite different in public than he is in private. His reputation and his true character should match.

3. Decide how the nominated names will be checked out. Probably the present elders should do this. The following steps should be involved: a. Discuss the eldership at length with the candidate, reviewing the responsibilities and qualifications, and picturing the job as a challenge, not as a snap. b. Discuss the eldership at length with the family of the candidate. c. If both the man and his family desire the job for him, set a period of time for them to be praying about the issue. d. Print the names of the candidates for the congregation's perusal ahead of election time and ask for any comments to be made privately to the elders. e. Follow up discussion on any comments received. f. If a man is found not to have the characteristics necessary for the job, explain to him that he will be protected if he would not pursue the office. g. Prior to the election, communicate with the congregation the procedures which have been followed in the selection of the candidates.

Who is to do the actual selection of the elders? It would seem best to have the entire congregation be a part of the final selection process. The leaders in Acts 6:1-6 were selected by the congregation. The statement that elders were "appointed" (Acts 14:23; Titus 1:5) has led some to believe that an individual or a small group out of the congregation did the selecting, but the texts do not enforce that interpretation. The Greek word for "appoint" (cheirotoneo) in Acts 14:23 literally means to choose by "raising the hand." It was commonly used to refer to people who raised a hand to express agreement in a vote. The word used in Titus 1:5 (kathistemi) does not preclude the choice by the congregation.

There are several questions about the selection of the elders that the Scriptures do not answer. Thus, we have flexibility and freedom in this area. We are not told in the Bible *how many* men to select. Too many times the number is decided and printed in the by-laws before the functions of the eldership are considered. It is erroneous to determine the number by how many can efficiently conduct business in a monthly board meeting. It would probably be best to select every man who has the qualifications and the desire to serve in this slot. Surely there are enough sheep to shepherd if each man who was qualified were to be chosen. The men who are this spiritually mature do not come in enormous bunches; but the higher the number of shepherds, the fewer sheep each one would be responsible for and the more people could be built up and developed to do the work of the church.

The Bible does not tell us *how long* a man should remain an elder. The churches have the freedom to require a man to drop out of the eldership for a time, perhaps to give him a rest and prevent "burn out." But an arbitrary rotation without regard for the benefit of the man or church smacks of the "corporation mentality."

The Bible does not tell us what to do if no man in the congregation qualifies for the eldership. When this happens, the various aspects of the shepherding functions need to be delegated to persons who can function in those ways. A committee could be chosen to do the delegation. While the absence of one qualification may prevent a person from serving in one way, other qualifications will enable him to serve in other ways. (In fact, when there are elders, they should be utilizing people to work in the areas in which they have ability and expertise. Every member in the church should be involved in meeting needs.) In matters of doctrine or discipline, elders from another church could help in the oversight.

What about the preacher's being an elder? Of course, he can be one if he meets the qualifications, desires the job, and is elected by the congregation. Peter was an elder (1 Peter 5:1). However, it would be important not to select him just because he was the preacher. It would be improper to expect a young man who recently graduated from college to function as an elder. Yet many preachers are expected to function as elders whether formally selected or not; consequently, he becomes not only an evangelist, but an elder as well (or pastor). Some preachers even call themselves *the* pastor. Young men do not have the maturity necessary to become *the* shepherd, and the church should not expect them to function as one. Many men have been frustrated in the ministry because of a congregation's insistence that they perform functions for which they are not ready.

Instead, may the young preacher and the older elders work together and help each other. The preacher can lead in Bible studies, preach, and perform the other duties for which he was trained. The elders can, in turn, help develop the young man into eldership material. Each should help the other develop in each other's abilities and responsibilities. The preacher should help elders to preach and elders should help preachers to shepherd in other ways.

How can the elders help develop other men to become elders? Here are some suggestions:

1. Work with the fathers and husbands to help to be better leaders at home; perhaps seminars, retreats, and encouraging the reading of good books would be helpful.

2. Each elder should consider choosing from the congregation another man, who is not an elder, to help him as he performs his functions.

3. Delegate some shepherding functions to others who have the interest and ability.

4. Elders should have a certain number of under-shepherds or deacons who work with them in various capacities.

SUMMARY

Since a congregation cannot rise beyond her leaders, she must choose those leaders who will bring the congregation closer to Christ-likeness. Such a task cannot be taken lightly.

CHAPTER TWELVE

OTHER GIFTED SERVANT-LEADERS

Although the continuing leadership ministry of the church includes evangelists and pastor-teachers (elders), it is not restricted to these two. There are at least three other categories of servant-leaders that we need to discuss.

DEACONS

The English word *deacon* comes from a Greek word that literally means *servant (diakonos)*. It is usually translated by either the word *servant* or *minister*. It is only one of several Greek words for servant. While all the words for servant emphasize subjection, this particular Greek word also underscores personal service rendered to another, usually with humility. It was first used to describe someone who waited tables for someone else. It was then expanded to describe all kinds of services rendered to another. In short, this kind of person was known to be "serviceable."

Diakonos is used twenty-nine times in the New Testament and refers to several different people:

1. Ones who seek greatness (Matthew 20:26; 23:11; Mark 9:35; 10:43).

2. Attendants at a banquet (Matthew 22:13; John 2:5, 9).

3. One who provided care to Jesus (John 12:26).

4. Government officials (Romans 13:4).

5. Jesus (Romans 15:8; Galatians 2:17).

6. A woman (Romans 16:1).

7. Apostles (2 Corinthians 3:6; 6:4; Ephesians 3:7; Colossians 1:23, 25).

8. Preachers and teachers (1 Corinthians 3:5; 2 Corinthians 11:23; Ephesians 6:21; Colossians 1:7; 4:7; 1 Timothy 4:6).

9. Disguised workers of the devil (2 Corinthians 11:15, twice).

10. A group of men chosen to serve with the elders (Philippians 1:1; 1 Timothy 3:8-13, twice).

The verb form of this word is used primarily, but not totally, to describe taking care of someone's physical needs in a general way (Matthew 4:11; 27:55; Mark 1:13; 15:41; Luke 4:39; 8:3; John 12:26; Acts 19:22; 2 Timothy 1:18; Philemon 13; Hebrews 6:10) and in the following specific ways: a. providing or serving food (Matthew 8:15; 25:44; Mark 1:31; Luke 10:40; 12:37; 17:8; 22:26, 27; John 12:2; Acts 6:2); b. providing friendship to a stranger (Matthew 25:44); c. providing clothes to the naked (Matthew 25:44); d. caring for the sick (Matthew 25:44); e. providing care to prisoners (Matthew 25:44); f. providing monetary relief (Romans 15:25; 2 Corinthians 8:19, 20). The verb also describes the activity of preaching (1 Peter 1:12; 4:10, 11), caring for spiritual needs or a combination of spiritual and physical needs (Matthew 20:28; Mark 10:45; 2 Corinthians 3:3; 1 Peter 4:10, 11), and exercising the "office" of the deacon (1 Timothy 3:10, 13).

A study of both the noun and the verb forms suggests that the category of leaders called "deacons" worked with the elders in meeting needs of people. Their role placed a heavy emphasis upon meeting physical needs (although it was not restricted to that). The Bible is silent concerning the specific functions of this group of leaders. They are mentioned as a group only three times, and always in connection with elders (Philippians 1:1; 1 Timothy 3:8-13, twice). Many scholars believe the first deacons were the seven men selected by the congregation to care for widows with no food provisions (Acts 6:1-6). Although we cannot be certain that they were the first literal "deacons" who were actually called that name, the situation of that selection probably gives us our best dynamic model for having deacons today.

The situation in Acts 6 was this: the apostles were not only leading in preaching, teaching and prayers, but also in the benevolent work of caring for widows. When that benevolent work grew to such proportions that the apostles had little time left for the ministry in the Word and for prayers, seven men were selected to look after the widows.

That principle should probably be followed today. Elders have the responsibility of the total shepherding activities of the church. However, they cannot *do* the total shepherding themselves. Every Christian is to be a servant of Christ by helping to meet the needs of other people. However, there comes a time in the life of a congregation that certain people need to be selected to insure that the needs of the people are taken care of. The initial group are the elders. As the needs increase, another group needs to be selected—the deacons. Deacons are selected servants—not to take away the service from the other members, but to help insure that service is not neglected. Deacons represent the whole congregation in specified kinds of services.

Rather than select deacons for a specified amount of time, it is probably better to select them for a specified task, such as benevolence, counseling, and absentee calling. There should be no deacons if there is no specified service for them to perform.

The Bible does not tell us how to select the deacons. If the seven in Acts 6 were deacons, the entire congregation selected them. However, it may become too cumbersome to have a congregational election every time deacons are needed for new or expanded needs that emerge. Thus it might be wise for the shepherd-elders to be free to select some deacons between elections. This is especially important in areas where congregations grow rapidly. The methods of selection are not as important as the reasons for the selection—that is, defined tasks. Selections should be made only after looking at both the specific tasks to be done and the qualifications of the men (1 Timothy 3:8-13). Because the deacons assist the elders, they also need a shepherd's heart. That is probably why some of the qualifications dovetail with those for elders. We could call the deacons "under-shepherds."

There is no Biblical hint that deacons were selected to vote on issues in some kind of board meeting. They are called servants, not voters. To restrict deacons to a place of status that gets fully carried out in a monthly meeting is erroneous. To help avoid such a misunderstanding, it might help to call the deacons servants or ministers (which is what the word really means). To call them ministers would help communicate the idea that the congregation does not have one minister, but many.

TEACHERS

Teachers are other gifted leaders in the ministry of the church (Acts 13:1; Romans 12:7; 1 Peter 4:10, 11). While elders are to be "apt to teach," they cannot do all the teaching. Thus, teachers assist the shepherds by communicating the Word to the members in an understandable and exciting way. As with the deacons, there is no hint in the Bible that the teachers were to vote on special issues at a board meeting.

The word teacher (didaskolos) is used in the New Testament to refer to Jesus (Matthew 8:19 and forty-five other verses), to Jewish leaders (Luke 2:46), Nicodemus (John 3:10), leaders in Antioch (Acts 13:1), Jews (Romans 2:20), Christian members (1 Corinthians 12:28, 29; Ephesians 4:11; Hebrews 5:12), Paul (1 Timothy 2:7; 2 Timothy 1:11), and deceivers (2 Timothy 4:3, 4).

The Scriptures do not outline how teachers in a congregation are selected. Congregations, then, have the freedom to be flexible in these matters. It would certainly be wise for elders to have significant input in the selection of the teachers. If not, the kind of care the shepherds are to give could be undermined by the teaching of the teachers. For instance, a teacher who does not believe the church should be involved in caring for the needs of people would stand in contradiction to the responsibilities of the shepherds.

Teachers may be the most influential group of people in the church, for they directly affect the minds of the members. While their selection is not mentioned in the Scriptures, we are told that some people will "accumulate for themselves teachers in accordance to their own desires" (2 Timothy 4:3). That is enough warning to suggest that someone besides the congregation at large should select teachers. We need to allow those who are mature in the faith and who are committed to the Word to select the teachers. That should not be done by asking for volunteers to teach. Instead, teachers should be sought. Inviting them to teach should be done by challenging them with what can be done and what a contribution they can make to the church.

Teachers need to continue their work by inviting others to help them in the classroom. Gradually the helpers can perform some of the teaching tasks, such as reading a story, giving an object lesson, or handling the visual aids. When the helper is mature in ability and confidence, he or she can teach the entire period.

Teachers must be able to control their tongues (James 3:1-11). They should be wise, have understanding, and demonstrate "by his good behavior his deeds in the gentleness of wisdom" (James 3:13). Teachers should be free of bitter jealousy, selfish ambition, and arrogance. They should be pure, peaceful, gentle, reasonable, full of mercy and good fruits, unwavering, and without hypocrisy (James 3:14-18).

HE WHO LEADS

Romans 12:8 mentions the third servant-leader in the church, "he who leads." The Greek word for *leads (proistemi)* is used only eight times in the New Testament. The "leader" so referred to may be 1. A gifted member in the body of Christ (Romans 12:8; 1 Thessalonians 5:12); 2. A man who manages his own household well—a home leader (1 Timothy 3:4, 5, 12); 3. An elder (1 Timothy 5:17); 4. A member who leads in good deeds (translated "engage in," Titus 3:8, 14).

"He who leads" is a general description of gifted leaders without putting a specific label onto them (Romans 12:8). The Greek word refers to leading with care, thus eliminating anyone who acts as a "bully." It could refer to those who motivate others and lead them in such activities as music, child care, or care for the elderly. Elders need to be on the lookout for persons with such leadership ability and interests. These leaders should also train others to lead out in ministries. Encouraging others to be motivators of people may be one of the most helpful things elders can do to spread out the shepherding tasks and expand the ministries of the church.

OTHER GIFTED PEOPLE

God never intended to dump the total ministry of the church onto one man or one small group in the church. He meant for every member to be involved in ministering within the family of God. A major function of the elders is to equip *every* member to minister (Ephesians 4:11-16). Each member has abilities that can be used for ministering to others (1 Corinthians 12:4-11; 1 Peter 4:10), and each member is important to the total ministry of the church (1 Corinthians 12:12-31; Romans 12:4-8).

Looking upon the church to meet the needs involves looking upon each individual member to discover what his contribution can be, equipping him, and using him. The leaders' work is never done until every person is involved in some kind of service (Ephesians 4:16). God has not left us ignorant about the kinds of people that are needed in the ministry of the church. The leaders must look for them. Here are some of the categories listed in the Scriptures of those people who are gifted by God to function in various ways:

1. *Helper* (1 Corinthians 12:28). This comes from the Greek word *(antilepsis)* that refers to someone who comes to the aid of another, one who helps someone else in his work. The "helper" may not be the person who first spots a need, or the person who decides how to meet that need, or the person who equips another to meet the need, or the person to motivate others to meet the need, but he or she will be the one who "takes up the matter" (another meaning of the Greek word) and helps meet the need. Often this person joins someone else who has taken the lead.

There are three ways these "helpers" can be described: a. Assistants to others. Many people do not feel competent in taking the lead in areas of ministry, but they are great helpers to others. Too many times, we have bypassed this important function. In one sense, these "helpers" are interns. Probably every Christian could be a helper alongside another Christian if we saw this as part of God's design for the church and were motivated to do it. We do this in Vacation Bible School and in the Bible School when we seek for assistants for the teachers, but it needs expansion into a true function in the church.

b. Those who "share in a task." These would work as co-partners for a specific task rather than as interns. Sometimes work gets delayed because too few people try to do it all by themselves. A person with a responsibility is wise to look for someone else to help him as a co-worker.

c. Those who help the needy. The needy could be someone like the poor, the orphans, or the widows. The help might include providing such necessities as clothing and food. The church has many people who may not be able to teach or counsel, but can help the needy. They should not be over-looked.

2. *Administrators* (1 Corinthians 12:28). This comes from a Greek word *(kubernetes)* which literally means a *steersman*. It referred to a ship's pilot or the one who takes the ship through the rocks to its goal. The same word was used in Acts 27:11 and Revelation 18:17. Various functions of the church need a pilot to help keep it on the track. Many shepherding responsibilities fail because someone with the ability to see that function through to the end has not been selected as the pilot. Many works within the church are done because people are administrators, although these people don't get much credit for it. They do not function to get honor, but to get jobs done. They are those who "pilot" the communion preparation, the baptismal preparation, the musical program, or the flower arrangements in the sanctuary, or those who see to it that there are ushers and nursery workers. This is certainly a much needed ministry and helps the programs of the church to run smoothly.

3. *Encouragers* (Romans 12:8). "He who exhorts" is from a Greek word *(parakaleo)* that means someone who is called alongside another for the purpose of encouragement and support of that person. These are the people who spur others on. Elders are to be encouragers, but they cannot do all the encouraging in the congregation. There are certain people in

every congregation who perform this function well. They may help parents who have mentally or physically handicapped children, comfort those going through periods of grief, help single parents, help troubled youngsters, or reach out to the elderly. Elders should always be alert to those who have this type of capacity and warmth of personality, and enlist them to be involved in ministries of encouragement.

4. *The Givers* (Romans 12:8). Of course, every Christian is to share financial resources for the work of God's church, but some people are gifted with a disposition for giving. This disposition is not necessarily connected with their monetary wealth; some of the poorest may be the most liberal givers. They don't need emotional appeals, special campaigns, or recognition in order to be moved to share. Shepherd-elders are to be willing to sacrifice, but they are not expected to do all the supporting of the church with their giving. When needs arise that call for special financing, the wise elder should know who is gifted for this type of ministry.

5. *Doers of Mercy* (Romans 12:8). This is the person who "feels" with another person in his plight and then acts accordingly. This is primarily benevolent work. Jesus expressed deeds of mercy to the hungry, the blind, the epileptic, the leprous, and those in financial distress. While some people may not be motivated to teach a Sunday School class at the church, they may be the ones who act quickly and appropriately when someone needs help.

SUMMARY

The shepherd-elders have the oversight or responsibility for the total ministry or program of the church, but each of these other leaders plays a vital part in the actual carrying through of the various areas of ministry. Each part functions in cooperation with every other part to build up and contribute to the whole in unity and harmony so the whole body can grow and mature to the stature of Christ (Ephesians 4:16). It is essential that the church plan for and realize the importance of the elders and all the other leaders—the evangelists, the deacons, the teachers, those who lead, the helpers, the administrators, the encouragers, the givers, and the doers of mercy. The governing of the church is not for the purpose of control, but for utilizing the many talents and interests of its members to fulfill the total work of the Lord.

CHAPTER THIRTEEN

STRUCTURING FOR SHEPHERDING

HINDRANCES

One hindrance to elders' being able to function as shepherds is the independent attitude of people. Many people do not want to be looked upon for the purpose of being cared for. This is especially true in the United States, where people have learned to take pride in pulling their own strings. We somehow think that to need help is to be weak and inferior, to be subhuman. Yet needing help is one of the most human characteristics there is. We begin life needing help. No infant can survive without personal care, and none of us outgrows the need for caring and loving. Not only is this true in the human family; it is also true in the family of God.

Although each member in the church is connected to the Head, Jesus, each member is held together by the support of fellow members. Every member is "fitted and held together by that which every joint supplies, according to the proper working of each individual part . . ." (Ephesians 4:16). One of the basic concepts that early Christians held on to was the need for and participation in fellowship (Acts 2:42).

Yet even in the first century, the independent spirit was present. Paul had to deal with it often. In doing so, he reminded the people of their need for one another (Romans 12:5, 10, 16; 13:8; 14:19; 15:7; 16:16; 1 Corinthians 12:12-27; Galatians 5:13; 6:2; Ephesians 4:2, 32; 5:21; Colossians 3:13; 1 Thessalonians 4:18; Hebrews 10:24). It is important always to keep before the members of any congregation the fact that Christianity involves the relationships of care, love, discipline, and submission for the purpose of helping one another. Any person who wants to be united to Jesus but does not desire to participate in the church is not ready to embrace Jesus or the new community of God's family.

Another hindrance to shepherding is the difficulty the elders have in discerning the needs of the people. Elders are not required to have ESP; thus, they cannot always pick the signals that someone sends out when he has a need. The elder's failure to meet needs may not be because he lacks compassion, but because of a lack of communication. People with needs should communicate their needs to the elders. This can be done by telephone, by speaking openly about it in a Bible School class, by a one-to-one discussion with an elder, in a sharing or prayer time in the church assembly, or through the church paper. I know of one particular congregation that publishes in its paper a column called the "Grapevine," in which is reported news of the members' activities, as well as their needs (such as when someone needs a baby-sitter, a plumber, or a musical instrument, or when they have something to share or sell).

We also need to try to be more sensitive to those who indirectly tell us they have needs—by the questions they ask, by their facial expressions, by their complaints, or by their body movements when a certain subject is discussed. There are also aspects of need that we should think of when certain situations arise. During a sickness, we should find out about the house and the meals, the care of the children, the medical bills, and the insurance. In the occurrence of death, we should inquire about financial needs because many times the bank account is frozen and the family has no cash. When unemployment arises, we should find out about the financial needs, check with employers within the congregation to see whether any jobs are available, and see whether any unpaid bills need to be paid. When there is only one parent in the home, either temporarily or permanently, there will be special needs in the home, such as preparing meals, doing laundry, cleaning, mowing the lawn, helping in transportation, and making home repairs.

Some people are too shy to communicate needs directly, or when they try, they don't make their needs clear. Thus, some elders may need to probe a bit. This is not being nosy; this is being loving. Sometimes close friends of the person in need are a good source if the person is reluctant to talk to an elder. However it is communicated, it should all be done in confidence. There is no need to make a big public display out of someone's need.

Another hindrance to shepherding is sometimes the traditional structure of the church. Someone recently said to me, "A shepherding program can never work in a church. I have set up several, but they all flopped. People are just too busy to be related to a specific flock with a shepherd." But when I asked if he had made any attempt to alter some of the traditional forms in order to institute the shepherding approach, he answered negatively.

The leadership in every congregation needs to ask two questions: (1) What is our present structure allowing us to do? and (2) What is our present structure preventing us from doing? The church has the freedom to structure for shepherding, and we ought to experiment with that freedom. There is no Biblical mandate that tells us how the Bible School, the worship services, or the midweek services are to be structured. There is not even any command that we have to have a Sunday night service or a midweek service. There is no command about what time of day we must meet for worship. We have the freedom to decide to meet in the afternoon or the evening if that would meet more of the needs of the people. We are to structrue our programs in order to allow for proper shepherding, not to maintain the status quo or to do what all other congregations do. And we should never let the attitude of "we have never done it that way" stop us from seeking to meet the needs of the people in the best possible way. Instead, we should always be asking, "Are we doing what the Lord would have us do?" God's will should take precedence over any details of structural form.

A POSSIBLE STRUCTURE

Any structure or organizational form should exist for one reason only—to help us be the church God intended us to be and to do what God intends for us to do. "Let the church be the church" is the motto for the structuring. Following is a description of one structure and how it could be used in order to evangelize and to take care of the church members.

a. *Shepherding groups.* One of the basic needs of an elder, in order to shepherd properly, is a defined flock. How can he be a shepherd unless he has some particular sheep for which to be responsible? It is quite practical to divide the congregation of family units and individuals among the elders. Yet it is not as easy as it sounds. Simply dividing up the congregation and sending out the announcement to the elders and the members may not benefit anyone but the paper company.

Do not obtain a copy of a successful shepherding program that another congregation has used and then expect it to be successful in yours. Learning from other congregations is valuable, but learning through a sheet of paper is insufficient. The learning process should include visiting that congregation, seeing the program in action, and even talking with those involved about the rewards and problems of it.

The way the flocks are grouped is important. One approach is to group those who live in a similar geographical area, making it easier for the elder to reach them and perhaps easier for the flock to fellowship. Another approach is to use an already established group, such as a Bible School class, as the flock; but we must be careful not to divide up family units.

Educate the entire congregation well in advance and in a comprehensive way about the nature of the church, the nature of leadership, the purpose, qualifications, and functions of the leaders, the Biblical model of the shepherd, and the ministries of each member before dividing into groups. To help the shepherd-elders, select men who can serve as "undershepherds" to help oversee smaller groups of members within the large fold or flock. They can help with the communication and the spotting of needs. They can prepare funeral meals, do hospital calling, minister to the sick, tutor failing students, and much more.

b. *We must program for fellowship.* People need to know each other in order to care for one another and feel that they belong to a flock. Time to be together for fellowship is a difficult problem in our fast-paced, multi-interested society. But the church can be flexible and creative in making fellowship possible. Occasionally, the flocks could meet with their shepherd-elders during the Bible School hour. Each elder could teach his class, and then the flock could be divided into groups of adults and children for fellowship and more teaching with the under-shepherds in charge. It is important that the children are included in the activities so that they feel they belong and can get to know the other adults and children in the flock.

Another way to enhance getting to know one another is having each of the flocks plan a Sunday evening program together and then present it to the whole congregation on a designated evening. This offers opportunities to find the talents and abilities of the members of the flock, for they should do the speaking, the song leading, the special music, the ushering, and whatever else they include in the service.

The flocks could also be made responsible for various ministries in the church. For instance, one flock could be responsible for the greeters and ushers for a month, one flock could call on newcomers in the community, another could do evangelistic calling or hospital calling, and on and on the list could go.

The Sunday evening hour could also be used for the flocks to meet. They could meet together in the church building or somewhere else to worship, to have a meal together, and to fellowship in other ways.

The flocks could have special retreats on a campground for a weekend or even for just a day. They could eat, study, and play together away from the rush and business of everyday life. Or the flocks could meet together in a park for swimming or group games and sports. This could involve such activities as boating, bicycling, hiking, fishing, and picnicking. A flock could go together to an amusement park, a sporting event, a special musical entertainment program, a seminar or conference, a convention, a nearby Bible college, or a museum.

The flocks could meet at the midweek time each week for a pitch-in meal and a devotional with a time for prayer requests and sharing. The shepherd-elder should teach or be in charge of the get-together. This type of meeting might be held in the homes. Or the flocks could meet at the church building for a prayer and praise time at least once a month instead of the midweek service. Having a sharing time and offering thanks for answered prayers would help everyone get better acquainted and informed of all the needs to be met. The people would discover whose grandmother was dying, who is getting a divorce and needs the church's help, who is entering college, who is sick at home with the flu, who is out of a job, and who has any other need. Many of these needs would not be expressed in the regular large assembly or formal worship service, but they might be in a small group.

The flocks could work together on a serving project, such as painting a widow's house, providing meals for a family who has experienced a death, mowing lawns for shut-ins or the sick, or helping a sick farmer.

All of these ideas are worth nothing if they are not adapted to the needs and time schedules of a particular congregation. We must not feel that we must do it the way it has been done in the past or that we cannot experiment with different ways to get the flocks to function well. We must not be so inflexible that we would never allow the midweek or Sunday night service to be dismissed so the flocks could meet. Because of the many different schedules of the members, we must be flexible enough to encourage the meetings of the flocks instead of discouraging them by having so many other church meetings on the calendar. Let's free the members to function as flocks instead of chaining them to a program.

c. *We must count the people.* We need to feel that each individual is a very special person, and we need to let each one know we think so by caring enough to miss him when he does not attend a service of the church. Each flock should decide together on how to follow-up on the absentees and then work their plan. The plan could involve the signing of attendance cards that are given to each shepherd-elder. The first time someone misses a service, the elder or an assistant could telephone him and say he was missed and ask if there is a need. If someone misses a second succeeding time, a member of the flock could visit. Every effort should be made to impress upon the missing member how much he is loved and missed. If he continues to miss repeatedly, perhaps a letter could be sent (after missing six weeks) asking for a response about that person's intentions concerning the church. If he continues to miss, explain that he is not considered a member of the flock any longer, but he would be welcome back anytime he wishes to return as a functioning member.

Of course, we should not be enslaved to a time schedule or a method in dealing with absentees. Each situation is different, and we must be flexible enough to adjust and be certain we are sincerely seeking to help the absentees with their needs.

d. *We must involve all the members.* Since every member has abilities to use for God, and since the church functions properly only when each member is doing his part, it is imperative that we help and encourage each member to make his or her contribution. Such involvement and a feeling that responsibilities are fulfilled are essential to each member's mental happiness and personal development.

As the flock meets together, abilities will become clear. As they are discovered, the shepherd-elder should be made aware of them, and they, in turn, should make the other elders aware. The elders will then inform the particular ministry in the church of what potentialities are available in their respective flock members.

It is devastating to be talented in a certain area but not be able to use it in the church. The shepherd-elder should see himself as "placement servant" who will not be satisfied until each member in the flock is given an opportunity to get involved in the church's ministry and use his or her abilities and interests.

THE ORGANIZATIONAL CHART

We usually think of an organizational chart as a piece of paper that tells us the chain-of-command and who is the boss. But since the church is not a business or a corporation, its organizational chart should display how the total work is being done and how all the various ministries are connected together in fellowship, cooperation, and unity with Jesus and His purposes. (See the Appendix, at the end of this chapter.)

As the Head of the body, Jesus is interested that many needs are met—evangelism, teaching, fellowship, worship, encouragement, care for the needy, and involvement in the community. He meets those needs through the functioning of the members of His body. He does not expect them to do it totally on their own, either; He equips them with the interests and abilities that are necessary to accomplish His purposes.

THE OFFICIAL BOARD

How does the official board fit into the structure? Probably more services have been either freed up or fettered down by official board members than anyone can even imagine.

The New Testament does not mention any church in the first century as having a board, but it is too cumbersome to bring every item before the entire congregation for a vote. There are detailed decisions that have to be made, and someone has to make them. However, the purpose and the limits of the board must be carefully thought out and communicated to the congregation and the board members. It is unwise to give the board powers to plan or execute the total church program when the board is dominated by people who do not have a shepherd's heart or mentality. Instead, the board should be the catalyst, the encourager, and the enabler for the shepherding of the members to take place.

The official board should be concerned about two main areas: (1) business of a material nature, such as finances and property, and (2) services of a personal nature—the meeting of the needs of the people. These two areas should not be seen as competitive. Every matter of a material nature should be looked at with a view of what will best help the people and their ministries.

The elders should probably make up the membership of the official board (but there are no biblical teachings that demand it). Otherwise, the shepherding interests might be ignored. Yet the elders should not get bogged down in minute decisions that certain members of the congregation could be trusted to handle in accordance with their abilities and interests.

When the board thinks it has to approve every little decision, its oversight becomes "snoopervision," takes priority over shepherding, and causes trust and development of people to decline. People become fettered rather than freed to serve in creative ways. The board should trust the people more and delegate responsibility. In that action, the board can be the coordinator rather than the controller. For example, the ministry of certain members is to take care of the physical property of the church building and grounds. The board should let them make such decisions about what material to purchase, whom to contact to repair the plumbing, when to mow the yard, and what shrubs to plant. The people in each area of service should know how much money they can spend and be trusted to spend it wisely. To have to approve every expenditure is to treat brothers and sisters in Christ as inferior children who cannot think or act without "snoopervision."

This is not to say that there should be no oversight at all. The less experience a person has with a given responsibility, the more oversight he needs to develop his abilities—but he does not need overbearing controls. Oversight given properly protects a person and serves to build him up so he will develop self-confidence. This type of oversight includes encouragement, support, love, assistance (helpers), and fellowship.

Perhaps the term "official board" could be dropped completely. The board should be made up of helpers or servants, not officials. To be more Biblical, we could call it simply "a meeting of the shepherds."

The shepherds do not *have* to meet every month. Becoming a slave to a meeting time, regardless of the need, lends itself more to the "snoopervision" mentality than one of service. But the size of the congregation and the number of functioning leaders will determine how often they need to meet.

PAYING THE SHEPHERDS?

Many congregations may discover that some shepherds should be paid. This is Biblical and ethical:

"Let the elders who rule well be considered worthy of double honor, especially those who work hard at preaching and teaching. For the Scripture says, 'You shall not muzzle the ox while he is threshing,' and 'The laborer is worthy of his wages.' " (1 Timothy 5:17, 18)

Some shepherds may feel a need to take time away from their wage-earning activities to care for the needs of the church. Such men should be paid; for they are not only to care for the church, they must also care for their own families. The church should be as concerned about the latter as about the former. I know of congregations that have fully-paid elders who are real blessings to them.

FAMILY LIFE OF THE SHEPHERDS

It is easy for a committed shepherd in the church to neglect his own family. We have urged some shepherds to do that by promoting the slogan, "The church first; family second." But the relationship of the church and the family cannot be described in such terms as first or second. Such ideas draw a line of demarcation between and encourage competition between the two institutions. Instead the relationship should be described as a circle connected together for the same purpose of serving Jesus, the Head of both:

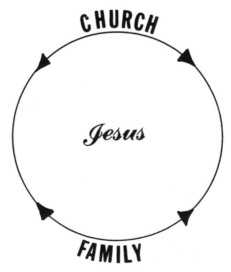

This idea stresses cooperation, unity, and interdependence between the church and the families. The church needs the family, and the family needs the church. The Bible often uses the same terms to describe both types of human relationships. Consider these: bride, children, birth, adoption, father, brothers, sisters, and household. And both the church and family are to be committed to the same values and principles, including faith, hope, love, discipline, and fellowship. The church and the families also share the same members. The members of my family are also people in the church. Thus, when a shepherd is doing something with his family, he is also doing something with a portion of the church. He is also the leader of the small group known as his family and has responsibility for them. His family could be called his "discipling" group.

A leader should not feel guilty if he has to say no to a responsibility in the church in order to say yes to the responsibility of his family. That is not being selfish, but wise. Actually it may be more selfish always to say yes to the church and to neglect the family at home because of the public recognition and the strokes that one's ego can receive from work in the church.

A balance in the two relationships is needed. A Christian shepherd who spends no time with his family is actually hurting the church (as well as himself) more than his services are helping. The children he neglects in his own home may cause the church to spend more time ministering to them in the future than would have been necessary if he had ministered to them as a father at home. Perhaps the greatest test of a man's real leadership is not in his ability to be flexible with the structures in the church, but with the structures in his own family. Real shepherding happens at home—first.

APPENDIX

Chart 1. This chart shows the relationship of Jesus, the Chief Shepherd, who looks upon and cares for the various needs of the people by having human shepherds meet people's needs and enlist others to help in that ministry. Thus all the members of the body pool their abilities and resources to meet the needs of each other. They are connected to each other by their belief in Christ and their love for one another and are connected to God by Jesus, His Son. They act as a unified whole, carrying out the concerns of the elders and relating to each other by fellowship, love, peace, edification, prayer, the apostles' doctrine, partnership, grace, and faith. There is no competitive spirit and no line-up of who is superior and who is inferior—all are equal, though they have diversity in abilities and needs.

Chart 2. This chart displays the various areas of service and how they flow into the overall purpose of meeting people's needs. Each area of service is an expression of the shepherds' concern for the people. Though varied, each area is related to every other area. None is more important than any other area.

Charts 3 and 4. These charts suggest ways the program of the church could be designed, proceeding from the general to the more specific.

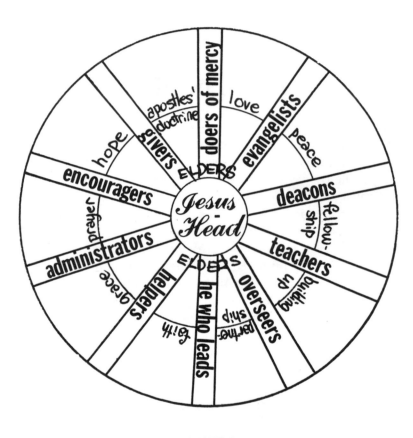

CHART 1

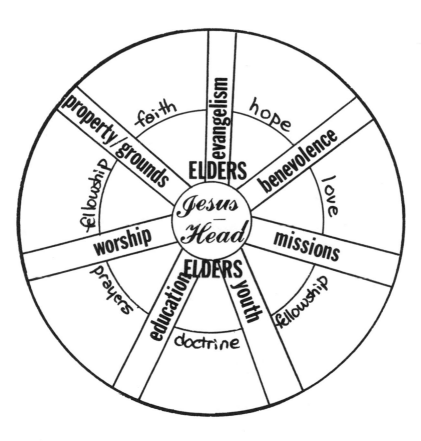

CHART 2

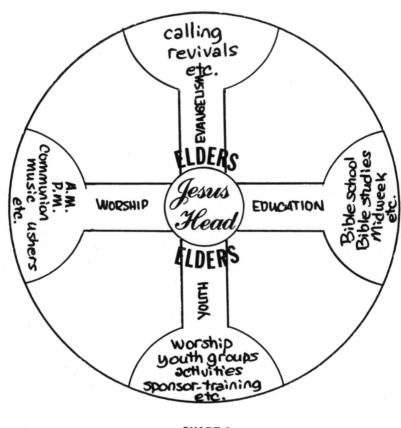

CHART 3

EDUCATION

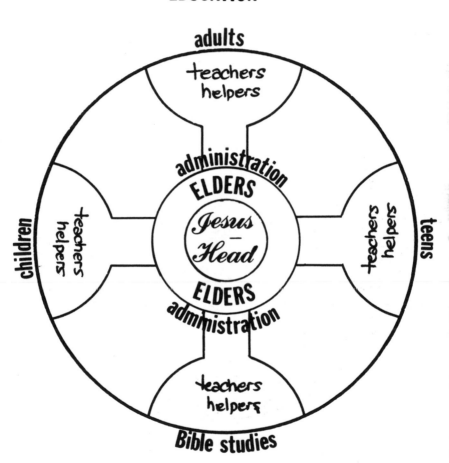

CHART 4

Textbooks by Standard Publishing:

The Christian Minister
  Sam E. Stone
Introduction to Christian Education
  Eleanor Daniel, John W. Wade, Charles Gresham
Ministering to Youth
  David Roadcup, editor
The Church on Purpose
  Joe Ellis

Commentary on Acts
  J. W. McGarvey
The Equipping Ministry
  Paul Benjamin
Essays on New Testament Christianity
  C. Robert Wetzel, editor
The Fourfold Gospel
  J. W. McGarvey and P. Y. Pendleton
The Jesus Years
  Thomas D. Thurman

How to Understand the Bible
  Knofel Staton
Teach With Success
  Guy P. Leavitt, revised by Eleanor Daniel

Available at your Christian bookstore or

More Books for
Christian Growth
by Knofel Staton

Grow, Christian, Grow. The spectacular stories of some very unlikely New Testament persons and how they grew spiritually. A challenging elective study for young people and adults.

How to Know the Will of God. What is God's will? How can you find out what He wants you to do? There are ways of finding God's guidance for the problems of everyday life. Some of them are presented in this book.

How to Understand the Bible. Easy-to-use Bible study tools for the layman. Step-by-step lessons, plus discussions of topics, words, customs and contexts. For individual or class study.

Check Your Lifestyle. Step-by-step guidelines on how to make the principles of Proverbs come to life in the 20th century. A painfully practical book that moves Christianty into the "nitty-gritty" of daily living. For class or individul study.

Check Your Character. A soul-searching study of the Beatitudes—"the beautiful attitudes of Jesus"—in the Sermon on the Mount. The Beatitudes explain Jesus' sometimes perplexing behavior. And they explain the rightness of the same behavior for us, for today. Each chapter ends with questions to check your motivations, your deepest thoughts, your basic attitudes.

Check Your Discipleship. A challenging consideration of Jesus' disciples and discipleship methods with application for today. Helpful for both disciple and discipler. Instructor's Guide contains discussion questions and "Getting Personal" questions for each chapter.

Available at your Christian bookstore or

STANDARD PUBLISHING